Praise for *Homesch*

"*Homeschool Rising* is just what parents need as they jump headlong into the adventure that homeschooling can be. Christy-Faith is a natural encourager who backs it all up with sound research and a warm heart for the parents she knows will benefit from reading this timely book. Occasionally, we doubt our choices as parents, and this book provides the right combination of helpful reminders, new ideas, and the inspiration a homeschooler needs to see their child's education through to the end. It will be a welcome tool in the hands of any parent—whether they're already homeschooling or are just thinking about getting started."

—*Colleen Kessler, M.Ed., Author of The Homeschool Advantage: A Child-Focused Approach to Raising Lifelong Learners and Raising Resilient Sons: A Boy Mom's Guide to Building Strong, Confident, and Emotionally Intelligent Families*

"Every parent should read this book as they make educational choices for their children. Christy-Faith reminds us that we don't have to be fearful while we return to the roots of individualized education. Instead, we can confidently impact the future of our children one homeschool at a time."

—*Sarah Collins, MSOT, OTR/L, Owner of HomeschoolOT*

"*Homeschool Rising* is the comprehensive, well-researched encouragement I wish I had 15 years ago when I began homeschooling. With her vast experience in education, Christy-Faith dispels common misconceptions, equips parents, and sheds a bright light on the value and benefit of choosing the transformative educational path of homeschooling."

—*Marni Love, Certified Parent Coach and Homeschool Mentor*

Homeschool Rising

Homeschool Rising

Shattering Myths, Finding Courage, and Opting Out of the School System

Christy-Faith

JB JOSSEY-BASS™
A Wiley Brand

Contents

To the guy who is the best decision I've ever made:
Scott, my best friend, the embodiment of humility,
unwavering support, and the best husband and dad
I've ever seen. Pinch me.

Author's Note

Names and identifying details of certain individuals mentioned in this book have been changed to protect their privacy.

Foreword

by **Brian D. Ray, Ph.D.**

Christy-Faith, in *Homeschool Rising*, goes near-surface, mid-depth, and deep in a balanced symphony that will engage and enhance the palate of every reader. The story line and history lesson simmers, rumbles, crescendos, and resolves, if you will read, listen, and heed. Are you a doubter of homeschooling? A negative critic? An enthusiast? Or one on the fence? Whichever you are, this book is for you. It is really a book about philosophy, practice, and thinking on the education of children and adults, despite its focus on parent-directed family-based education.

I was educated at home and in 12 years of Roman Catholic schools. I was an eager learner and an academic achiever and went on to a B.S. in biology, an M.S. in zoology, a state-issued teaching certificate, teaching in private and public schools, and then on to a Ph.D. in science education. After that, undergraduate and graduate college/university teaching in sciences, research methodology, statistics, and the philosophy of education. I have taught hundreds of homeschool, public school, and private school students. Oh, and by the way, I have spent 39 years studying, doing research on, and publishing scholarly articles and books on homeschoolers and the home-education movement. I have been a part of many meetings and conferences within the homeschool community. Let me tell you, Christy-Faith hits it out of the ballpark with this book at every turn of the page.

Christy-Faith was institutionally schooled. She and her husband ran an education business helping children, of typically wealthy families, achieve, learn, and succeed in schools. Then they had an educational conversion experience and had their eyes opened about all manner of things education. Christy-Faith is witty and insightful. Her writing will grab you.

Homeschool Rising covers—respectfully, with gravitas, with grace, with careful circumspection, and without either sugar-coating or damaging the name and promises of parent-led home-based education—all the important topics. Christy-Faith plumbs the depths of many of the great names of the modern homeschool movement. She covers the pioneers and current important figures and their essential ideas. Christy-Faith gives attestation to and offers her readers the kernels of foresight and wisdom of these men and women. And she does it in a culturally relevant and engaging way for those living today. At the same time, her approach is timeless.

Christy-Faith also provides her readers the most current empirical evidence on this old and new form of education, homeschooling. Whether it is children's academic achievement, social and emotional development, the joy and love of learning, or their relative success in adulthood, Christy-Faith lays out the scholarly research findings in a fair and balanced way that will satisfy the academic in you.

A key thing that I appreciate about *Homeschool Rising* is that it does not leave its readers with a lackadaisical or nonchalant attitude of whatever, or what will be, will be. Is there good in the world? Is there anything noble? Is there anything about which we should think deeply? Does all of this relate to the education of our children? Do I truly believe that my children's education is at the core of life and I will give all that I can to it? Or, will I just jump on the cultural bandwagon and send him or her off to some conventional institutional school or some new alternative schooling (e.g., pod, micro school, tax-funded school at home, online virtual school, you name it) that is essentially under the grand influence, authority, and relationship of the government or some private group that is not related to my children? Christy-Faith will not let her readers off the hook on this one.

Does all of this really matter? Christy-Faith starts with and brings her readers to a resounding, YES! That is, dads and moms, grandparents, policymakers, professional educators, and everyday neighbors to everyday families must face the often-ignored fundamental realities about the educational upbringing of children. The education of children is crucial to the core of any family, community, society, and nation.

Christy-Faith encourages her readers to question the practice and authority of the normal way today. Ask how we got to the point of over 99.5% of children by the 1970s in the United States being taught, trained, and indoctrinated in institutional schools outside of any authentic influence of the parents and family. Question the expertise of the alleged experts. Dig deep into your own history and experiences with schooling. Look at this in light of the history of institutional schooling in other nations and the United States. Care more about your child's deep current and future life and learning than society's default setting, and open your eyes and ears to hear and understand why homeschooling is rising.

Christy-Faith comes from outside and now inside the homeschool movement and community. I learned from her that there are younger people like the pioneers of this 40-year-old, history-changing movement called "homeschooling," and she is one of them. Christy-Faith's multifaceted experience and insights are just what the world needs right now when it comes to understanding and appreciating parent-led family-based education. Whether you want to just dip your toes into the discussion or go deep, you will be glad you read this. And her book will stand the test of time.

Homeschool Rising, with Christy-Faith, will poke you, prod you, make you laugh, and bring you to face your deepest thoughts about education and schooling. She offers you anecdotes, empirical evidence, and emotional draws. Parent, doubter, enthusiast, and fence-sitter—Christy-Faith will educate, enlighten, and edify you if you will open a little crack of space in your mind and heart and let her in with *Homeschool Rising*.

> Dr. Brian D. Ray, founder and president of the
> National Home Education Research Institute
> October 3, 2023

Rethinking Childhood

The Most Dangerous Question: What Makes for a Great Education?

"To think critically, people must be motivated and free to voice their own ideas and to raise their own questions but in school students learn that their own ideas and questions don't count. What counts are their abilities to provide the correct answers to questions that they did not ask and that do not interest them."

—Peter Gray, from his book *Free to Learn*[1]

"Dad, puh-leeze!"

My 16-year-old self was screaming inside. I was struggling in physics, had a test tomorrow, and my grade was currently a *B*. Yes, the scarlet letter in my book: a *B*.

I had reached the limit of my own capacities and needed help. Kinematics was hard and I hate to admit this, but I hadn't even earned that *B*. I cheated my way there and finally reached the point where I could no longer fake it. I was in dire straits. After all, my GPA was at stake (a.k.a my whole future), and I needed help.

In comes Dad. Now, let me provide some context first. My dad isn't "normal." He's an actual genius, an engineer (more accurately, an inventor) who's won many awards for what comes out of his mind. He's the curious type when it comes to learning.

When I asked for help, I knew I needed to contain the situation because (cue the eye roll that didn't appreciate it at the time) he was going to become enthused about how cool kinematics is, start explaining superfluous abstractions and applications, and add on a side of tangents that would confuse even the kids I was cheating off of. We had to stay on track if I wanted ACTUAL help.

"The test, Dad . . . the test is TOMORROW! I don't need to know all this! Just tell me what I need to know to score well."

In that moment, the last thing I truly cared about was why this material matters, why it's interesting, and how it applies to our world. It was crunch time. To be completely honest, even if my transcripts weren't on the verge of becoming a complete dumpster fire (I did tend to catastrophize back then), I found myself utterly indifferent toward the subject matter. I knew I was never going to use this stuff again in my life. I was only taking the class to fulfill college prerequisites.

Understanding physics was my lowest priority; getting the grade in physics was the highest. That's the whole point anyway, isn't it? To play the game, get the grades, so you can get where you want to go? Of course, it is.

Chasing Grades

Through the years, I've seen this letter grade–chase play out over and over again. As the founder of one of L.A.'s most prominent learning centers, I remember having that

The Most Dangerous Question   **5**

conversation hundreds of times. A parent would hire our team to tutor their child. We would have only 50 minutes to work together, so the questions quickly became, "What do you need to know? What does the teacher want? How are we going to give them what they want to nail the right grade?"

Any excitement, interest, or even discussion about the material was nonexistent. Out the window. There was no time for anything but delivering what the teacher wanted.

It's the nonstop treadmill of grades and academic achievement (honor roll, anyone?) with the exhausting chase of looking *perfect* on your transcript for your dream colleges. The undercurrent of this letter grade–driven madness is anxiety, peer pressure, bullying, wearing the right clothes, the social environment, gobs of insecurities, and real dangers kids face in the traditional schooling system *every single day*.

> *The undercurrent of this grade-driven madness is anxiety, peer pressure, bullying, and real dangers kids face in the school system school every single day.*

How would I know? This was my story. Grades were everything to me growing up. I should clarify, though. Grades were everything for me starting in the *fourth grade*. Before that, I was a completely different girl.

The Dawn of Grade Perfectionism (and Performance Anxiety)

It wasn't until fourth grade that I even knew grades were a thing. I was given tests and didn't know it. I thought school was where you go to learn if you wanted to but no big deal either way. My older sister had profound learning challenges and my parents never spoke of grades in the house.

Educating my sister and navigating the school system during a time (the 1980s) when most administrators and teachers did not believe learning disabilities were real was an uphill battle. Getting my sister to learn was a constant trial, and the last thing my parents wanted to do was talk about grades around my sister. She was in and out of therapies for most of her childhood.

But one day, things changed.

My fourth-grade teacher told my mom in a parent-teacher conference that I was very smart but not living up to my potential. Apparently, I was getting Cs (I had no idea). Nor did I even know I was graded at this thing called school. But apparently, I was a smart girl who could be doing better. Or so my parents were told.

My parents did what most parents would do when confronted with this situation. They sat me down and told me I needed to get better grades. They showed me my report card (the first time I'd ever seen one) and told me Cs meant "average" and that I was capable of a lot better. That I could be getting As if I tried, and that A is the best grade.

They then laid out a plan to motivate me to get better grades. Money. That was it.

Apparently, they were right, I wasn't working to my potential because from that day forward, I got those As. Heck, yeah, I did. We didn't have a lot of money back then so to have cash was amazing. Here's how our deal went: if I went up a grade (so if I took a C to a B), I got $20, and once

I got that to an *A*, I would get $20 for keeping every *A*. My parents were not wealthy by any means, so I know that cash ($100 bucks give or take) every quarter was a lot for them. Overnight I became the student every teacher and parent wants. A straight-*A* poster child.

From. That. Day. Forward.

The Problem with the Plan

As I got older, though, what started as a rather innocent motivation for money turned into unhealthy perfectionism. I started to get praised for being smart by my parents and teachers, I started comparing my grades with my friends, and I started to tie my self-worth to my marks. Get the *A*? That means you're smart.

That means your teachers will like you. That means your parents will praise you to their friends. That means you are worthy.

I learned how to perform and deliver. I was doing this childhood thing correctly. My parents loved seeing my accomplishments, but I took this expectation to an unhealthy place. Why not? My school and teachers raved about my academic success. Applause is addicting, especially when you're great at playing to the judges.

This concept held tight as I entered the realms of college and graduate school. The objective was clear-cut: emerge from academia with an unblemished 4.0. It wasn't merely about showcasing intelligence; it was about securing the elusive key to unlocking my aspirations. Yet, beneath the surface of high grades, a more profound truth was taking shape. Behind the veil of flawlessness, there resided a girl carrying hidden scars, driven by an unspoken belief that perfect grades could mend the internal wounds.

In the midst of this narrative unfolding, my experience is far from isolated. What transpired in my journey resonates broadly among children who grapple not only with the pursuit of acceptance, but also with the subtle messages our education system imparts. This yearning runs deep, interwoven into the very fabric of our schools. It's nurtured by the notion that tangible achievements hold the key to future success. Within this intricate choreography, classrooms transform into stages, with assignments and tests as avenues to stand out, to matter. Beneath the pursuit of grades lies a delicate reality: the longing for self-worth entwined with external success. It's a narrative extending beyond my own, painting a poignant image of countless children seeking validation through academic accomplishments.

Back in fourth grade, I couldn't foresee this trajectory unfolding. At that moment, I was simply thrilled about the monetary reward. Little did I know, there was a lot more tied to those good grades. But in retrospect, something shifted within me during that fourth-grade encounter. Learning, with which admittedly I had only maintained a casual relationship until then, suddenly lost its significance.

Beneath the pursuit of grades lies a delicate reality: the longing for self-worth entwined with external success.

Following that meeting with my parents, I found myself spending the subsequent years of my academic journey being more interested in the act of securing good grades than in the actual material I was learning. The only "connections and deep thoughts" that mattered were the ones that impressed teachers, professors, and graduate advisors—all in the pursuit of securing that coveted grade. It wasn't about genuine engagement; it was about achieving the paper that validated an A, honors, or a Master's degree. I held the conviction that having those grades or that degree was a testament to my accomplishments, my knowledge, or more precisely, my identity.

Sad. Oh, how misinformed I was.

Perpetuating the Cycle

I carried this mentality into my adult years. I got a teaching job at a school in a wealthy area where the parents, too, cared about achievement. It was a match made in heaven. A driven type-A academic teacher pursuing her Master's teaching the kids of other "high achievers" how to go places.

Don't get me wrong, while growing up, I did have those occasional moments of true enthusiasm for learning that everyone desires. This is precisely why I chose a history degree over a possibly more lucrative career path. The idea that actual stories can be even more astonishing than fiction, along with the boundless wisdom we can gather by exploring the past, struck a chord with me.

Nonetheless, catching a glimpse of that "love of learning" within my studies was a rarity, as bunny trails were infrequent, and time was often limited. Such moments were only permitted (both by my choice and the unyielding demands of the system) if they aligned with my overarching goals—achieving top grades in pursuit of success.

As Denise Pope would say, throughout my years of studies I was "doing school,"[2] not really engaging or enjoying learning.

Fast-forward a decade.

I became so skilled at achieving, and I married a similarly driven achiever, Scott, which led us to build a flourishing business centered on children's accomplishments.

We helped kids who struggled to "achieve" when the schools failed them. We were hired to solve problems the public and private schools could not.

We did whatever it took to deliver. To get kids on track. To get them to learn. And we were good at it too. Our center was also different from many other learning centers in that we truly cared about each and every one of those kids who walked through our doors. Make no mistake, we were hired to get results, but at the same time, I was still the little sister to a girl who struggled tremendously to be able to learn. I wanted to help. Kids who came to us knew they were in a safe place, and we genuinely cared about helping them.

What if there is a better, healthier way to get this education thing done?

We worked with thousands of kids ranging from kindergarten through college from over 20 public and 30 private schools in our area. I spent my days training and managing my staff of specialists and tutors, pouring over Individualized Education Programs (IEPs), and discussing student needs with principals, admissions counselors, therapists, psychologists, and parents. We delivered highly individualized educational plans and impressive academic outcomes.

But . . . this wasn't my calling. There was more in store for me. After having my first child, I had an awakening. Through a series of conversations, tough introspection, and placing on the altar of uncertainty everything I *thought* I knew about education, it all came down to one key question: "What if there is a better, healthier way to get this education thing done?"

My Deconstruction Begins

I observed and participated in this grind that most kids in our country are forced to experience for decades. Go to school for seven hours a day just to come home and do several hours of homework in the evenings. When they're not doing homework, kids are shuttled around to adult-led extracurricular activities (organized sports are not play, by the way). Often, these kids leave their house at 7 a.m. and don't return until 7 p.m. or even later. Kids would show up at our center, dinners in hand, with their parents telling us, "Call us when they're done!" Looking around at our center with all these kids, while holding my own infant, I wondered, "Is this the future I want for my kid? This grind?"

In this pivotal moment of deconstruction, a torrent of questions flooded my thoughts: "What kind of childhood is being shaped here? What exactly propels our actions? Do our efforts genuinely make a difference, and if so, do they address what truly matters? Amid these pursuits, do these students experience moments of genuine joy? Can they carve out time for cherished family bonds? Are their passions acknowledged and embraced, or does the cease-less pace of their lives obstruct such pursuits?"

The scales started lifting from my eyes. I was heart-broken that kids in my center with real learning chal-lenges were at school all day just to be at tutoring and/ or receiving remediations all night. Not to mention week-ends. Throughout the day, at school, many of our students received signals that something was wrong with them or they were not smart enough or "needing extra help." Just to succeed they would come to our center after school and spend hours working with us to ensure they made decent grades. We also had the overachievers who needed As and came to us for AP Bio, Honors English (or whatever) so they could maintain their GPA to get that golden ticket of an acceptance letter from the school they "needed" to get into.

That awakening would forever change the trajectory of my life. Like, FOREVER. It led us to move states away and sell the business Scott and I built for over 17 years.

Finding Hope in Unexpected Places

As I mentioned before, we worked with a lot of kids at our center. Most students, if not all, were "doing school" to get it over with.[3] I can count on one hand the kids who actu-ally loved learning. Most everyone else—and I would argue this is true all across our country—views school as a neces-sary inconvenience. So many of our clients, kids and adults included, knew that much of what is learned in school has no relevance to real life.

Public school, private school, it doesn't matter; education in this country has largely been reduced to "going through the motions."

> *Education has largely been reduced to "going through the motions."*

What if we could do better? What if our kids could truly love learning AND be prepared for a successful life? What if we didn't have to choose one or the other? What if there is a better way than conforming to a system that many would agree is "smoke and mirrors"? What if we did something instead of watching as critical thinking and autonomy are further devalued?

That's where we brought in the two questions that inspired us to sell our business, relocate, and pursue homeschooling.

1. What makes for a great education?

2. Are schools achieving this?

Yikes.

The implications of pondering these questions are weighty. Just how big of a problem do we have on our hands?

And what does this have to do with homeschooling? Everything. Just sit tight.

And I know what you're thinking . . .

> "Sure, Christy, you may be able to convince me that home-schooling is a great option for families, but not everyone can homeschool."

Yes. I know.

And I will add to that . . .

Not everyone *should* homeschool.

That doesn't mean it's not a worthy topic to ponder, and possibly one of the most important matters to think about.

After all, we are talking about childhoods here. Where the majority of our kids spend seven-plus hours a day for 13 years straight. Ask any therapist and they will tell you that the childhood years, interactions with caregivers, parents, and their environments have a lasting impact on a child's emotional, social, and cognitive development. To raise children into healthy adults, it's crucial that they are provided with a safe, nurturing environment as they are growing up.

It's having the courage to truly ask ourselves, "This may be normal, but is this 'normal' good?"

Frederick Douglass spoke to the heart of the matter, "It is easier to build strong children than to repair broken men."[4]

That's what this book is about: rethinking childhood. Rather than accepting common practices as the right way to do things, instead, we're taking an inventory of our kids' growing up and being educated experiences. It's having the courage to truly ask ourselves, "This may be normal, but is this 'normal' good?"

The normal childhood in our culture is to send our kids away from their homes and into classrooms for seven-plus hours a day, five days a week until they are 18. To a place most kids hate.[5] To a place that often kills a love of learning (more on this later) and is unhealthy at best and toxic at worst socially (more on that later, too). We hand our kids over to people we don't know that well for a large majority of their growing-up years, for hours on end, and aren't allowed to see our children without permission. Yet, we don't think twice.

The irony is, most of our culture has zero hesitation when passively sending their children into this system every single day. After all, our kids need an education. And our government knows what they're doing so we can trust them to do it, right? A considerable number of people wish to believe that our government possesses the insight to champion our welfare and make prudent decisions for us, particularly in matters concerning our children's education. Nevertheless, the reality that many of us acknowledge is that this hope rests on an inherently unrealistic premise.

These are our kids. Our *precious children.*

You wouldn't let just anyone access your bank account without your approval, and yet, you're supposed to just give your kids over to complete strangers for 13 years!

However, this current structure hasn't always been the norm. While it's only about 150 years old in the larger history of education, it's crucial to recognize that throughout history, remarkable thinkers have pondered and envisioned education

The moment has arrived to liberate ourselves from the confines of the past century and a half and from the prevailing belief that schools hold unquestionable authority over our children's education.

in vastly different ways. Despite this, due to the weight of tradition and the fact that we've been immersed in the mass schooling system for two generations, many parents accept this arrangement without a second thought. It's almost as if we haven't been given a genuine choice because we're predominantly familiar with only one approach. Nonetheless, I firmly believe it's time to step back and rigorously assess its effectiveness and outcomes. The moment has arrived to liberate ourselves from the confines of the past century and a half and from the prevailing belief that schools hold unquestionable authority over our children's education.

Now, I need to say this before being misunderstood. I am pro-homeschooling. Yes, but I am pro-homeschooling because I believe children are persons who need to be honored and loved. Through my deconstruction journey into believing homeschooling is a legitimate and healthy way to educate kids, my heart aches because I know there are many kids in our country who would greatly benefit from being pulled from schools and educated in a loving and safe home who, sadly, never will. This is why I hold these truths together:

- **Truth No. 1:** Homeschooling goes beyond simply being a legitimate educational choice for families; it is also the best way to provide tailored academics, instill a love of learning, foster social/emotional health, and cultivate stronger family bonds.
- **Truth No. 2:** Not every child will get the educational experience that is available through home education (though I wish they could).

I have more than once been called out for not putting my efforts toward reforming the system. If homeschooling is as good as we say it is, it's not right that all kids won't get it.

The system is beyond reform. It is working exactly how it was intended.

I have concluded the system is beyond reform. It is working exactly how it was intended to work and because of circumstances beyond my control, I don't see this changing anytime soon.

And then, there is homeschooling.

From One Heart to Another

When it comes to discussing a child's education, we aren't talking about the pros and cons of something trivial like what jeans to wear or what to cook for dinner tonight—we are talking about entire childhoods. And childhoods matter. Kids matter . . . we are talking about entire childhoods. And childhoods matter. *Kids matter.*

If you are a current homeschooler who doesn't know what to do with the naysayers out in the world or the most powerful naysayer (the one in your mind), this book is for you. You may be asking, "Will I mess up my kids? How do I know if I'm doing enough?" My promise is you will finish this book with a renewed sense of purpose and unshakable confidence in your homeschooling choice.

> *. . . we are talking about entire childhoods. And childhoods matter. Kids matter.*

If you are a professional who works with kids, whether that be as a pediatrician, therapist, teacher, ministry worker, and so on who has valid concerns about homeschooling, I trust you will have an open mind. As Mary Lathrap conveyed in "Walk a Mile in His Moccasins"[6] (formerly, "Judge Softly") or as Brené Brown states in *Braving the Wilderness*, "People are hard to hate close up,"[7] I ask a favor. Will you lean in? Will you hear me out? You owe it to yourself to educate yourself on educational alternatives so you can better advise families. You owe it to the families you work with to advise them based on current, accurate information.

If you are one of the 11 million parents in America who are dissatisfied with the school system[8] but have yet to take the leap into this unknown world of home education, I can't wait to move you from "How do I even start?" to "I know I won't start perfectly, but it's better than what we're doing." No worries. I got you.

My promise is you will finish this book with a renewed sense of purpose and unshakable confidence in your homeschooling choice.

If you are a friend or family member who has some deep concerns about the well-being of your grandkids, nieces, nephews, god kids, or close friends, first, we need to acknowledge your care and love. I'm sure you have questions, "How will they be ready for college? How will they be socialized? Is it good to shelter kids like this? What about diverse social interactions? They don't look like they're learning what they are supposed to be learning . . ." I could go on and on.

I know your questions because I had them myself. Come, sit, and have coffee with me. No judgment here. Your genuine concern is commendable. The first thing I want you to know—from an educator who, for over 20 years, got kids perfect SAT scores, guided nonreaders to become readers, and helped land other kids in Ivy League schools—is that a great education doesn't need to look like what the schools are doing. The statistics show we are doing a much better job educating at home anyways; it will be okay. But you need convincing, I know. I'm here to show you the truth and the data to support it.

I was each of you. I was the skeptic who thought homeschooling was for weirdos or for fringe religious families.

I was the professional who thought homeschooling was okay only as a temporary solution but not a viable long-term alternative. I was the fearful mom who decided to do this but had zero guidance. I also was (and am) the home-school mom scared to death to mess this thing up.

In all my research and experience, I have concluded that your kids deserve better than what the schools can provide and that as a loving, motivated parent, you are the best person to give your kids the education they need to succeed. And that goes far beyond the letters on a report card.

This is the essence that underpins this book—an unwavering commitment to securing the best for our children's future. With this understanding in mind, we can wholeheartedly embark on this journey together. So, let's get after it.

> *This is the essence that underpins this book—an unwavering commitment to securing the best for our children's future.*

Remember This

- Students, as I did, learn to give up inquisitive learning for "doing school."

- Because we've been immersed in the mass schooling system for two generations, many parents accept this arrangement without a second thought.

- The best way to provide tailored academics, instill a love of learning, and foster social/emotional health is to homeschool.

CHAPTER TWO

The Homeschool Revolution: Why Parents Are Pulling Out Their Kids in Droves

"I never let my schooling interfere with my education."
—Mark Twain[1]

Homeschool Rising—you maybe questioned why this title for the book, why this idea sprawls across the screen or page you're staring at right now. For starters, a rising is often seen as a movement, the initial shift in momentum at a significant moment in history. The phrase "mercury rising" is a nod to the temperature rising in the now-extinct mercurial thermometers. It's a key inflection point for those who recognize the times we live in and know how to respond accordingly.

The heat is unquestionably on the traditional school system as more and more parents (and kids) are becoming increasingly disillusioned with America's default educational option. This 150-year-old exercise in intellectual conformity threatens to rob future generations of the ability to think critically and to engage with varying viewpoints.

21

Even the label itself—traditional education—confuses the conversation about what education truly is. Are the traditional system's results, experiences, and intentions worth carrying on for future generations?

There is a palpable shift in the conversation, the rhetoric, even the philosophy of what learning truly entails, a shift threatening to rightly expose the ideology and questionable intentions fueling this underwhelming, overreaching machine we call traditional education. That time is now with *Homeschool Rising*.

It's okay to admit skepticism, whether it's about homeschooling, reading a new report online, or even this book. That's a healthy perspective to maintain. It's also why I'm not asking you to simply take me at my word as to why the popularity of homeschooling is rising. What I am asking is for you to consider the mountain of evidence that shows why homeschooling is rising in the hearts and homes of more brave parents, caregivers, medical experts, mental health specialists, and countless others.

First, we need to recognize how much homeschooling has moved from being a fringe, freshly legalized form of education across the United States in 1993 to such a significant movement today. Homeschooling is quickly being a widely accepted form of education, sparking a fresh new who's who graduating from the ranks of homeschoolers.

The track record of world-changers who were homeschooled is staggering . . .

Thomas Edison, Abraham Lincoln, J.R.R. Tolkien, Soichiro Honda, Bill Lear, Andrew Carnegie, Leonardo da Vinci, C.S. Lewis, Teddy Roosevelt, George Washington

Carver, Sandra Day O'Connor, Dr. Willard S. Boyle, Erik Demaine, Margaret Mead, Erwin Schrödinger, and of course, Tim Tebow. All homeschooled.

Homeschooling is the fastest-growing form of school choice in the United States right now. According to the National Center for Education Statistics (NCES), during the 2019–2020 school year, approximately 49.4 million children attended public schools in the United States.[2] Private school students numbered approximately 4.7 million in that same school year.[3] Quickly climbing the ranks is the estimated 2.6 million students who are being educated at home.[4] What happened next was an awakening we have never seen before in the world of homeschooling.

The Seismic Shift of Enrollment from 2020 to 2021

Prior to the pandemic, the number of U.S. homeschooling households was about 3.23% of those with school-aged children.[5] This growth remained steady at about 3.3% per year until kids were brought home and took their classes virtually through Zoom and home computer screens. Parents got a much closer look at what their kids were truly learning in school—and they weren't happy, and sometimes downright appalled by what they saw.

What happened from the end of 2020 through the end of 2021 was the first seismic shift in the landscape of traditional education. U.S. Census data shows from spring *2020 to end of year 2021*, the number of U.S.-based families with school-age children that homeschooled increased to 11.1%.[6] This tripled the previous decade's average annual growth rate of 3.3%![7] The rising of homeschools is illustrated in the following chart, including the drastic jump in homeschools when parents saw firsthand what their child was being taught by their school system.

There is a shift to expose the questionable ideology and intentions fueling the underwhelming, over-reaching machine we call traditional education.

Families are seeing the signs of homeschooling rising in popularity, but the more pressing question is, "Why?" The data can't be dismissed as simply a pandemic-related anomaly. There is a multi-decade upward trajectory in the growth of homeschooling, accelerated by a global health crisis, that continues *after* students were welcomed back to in-person classes. Shifting geo-population patterns, birth rate variances, and

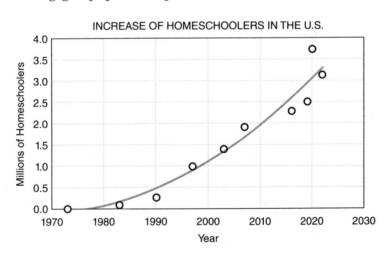

INCREASE OF HOMESCHOOLERS IN THE U.S.

FIGURE 2.1 A dramatic rise in homeschooling

Source: https://www.nheri.org/research-facts-on-homeschooling/

life transitions cannot possibly explain away such a shift. Maybe, just maybe, it's because families are seeing behind the curtain. And exactly who are these families making the leap into homeschooling?

Who Are the New Faces of the Homeschooling Movement?

If someone 20 years ago asked you to describe what a homeschool family looks like, you probably had a specific profile in mind. You probably pictured a white, middle-class family, Christian, several kids, conservative in their values, political affiliations, and practices.

The long-held stereotype of homeschooling families as white, middle-class, and Christian is changing. Homeschooling is becoming a mainstream option for many families who are fed up with increasingly standardized mass schooling.

Consider these stats that reflect the growing diversity of homeschooling:

- 25% of homeschool families are secular (i.e., nonreligious).[8]
- 41% of homeschooled students are Black, Asian, Hispanic, and others (i.e., not White/non-Hispanic).[9]
- A near five-fold increase in homeschooling black families from 3.3% to 16.1% in 2020.[10]

> *"But, Christy, you've shown me trends and evidence of this movement growing, but you still haven't explained why homeschooling is on the rise."*

You're right, and there's a reason. This whole conversation up until now is showing you that you're not alone in your questions and maybe even your dissatisfaction.

Why is homeschooling gaining so much popularity? Because the traditional school system has failed, and continues to fail families in five key areas:

1. Child safety

2. Mental health

3. Academic proficiency

4. Family dynamics and key relationships

5. The overall well-being of the child

Let's begin . . .

Traditional Schooling Is Culpable for the Death of Thousands of Children and Teens Every Year

You don't need me to convince you how dangerous traditional schools are nowadays with increased gun violence and unchecked risks to students and educators alike. I cannot fathom the sheer terror that goes through the hearts and minds of parents whenever they get *that* call: another school shooting. I remember the first time I saw bulletproof backpacks for sale on Amazon. This isn't right! Soldiers, law enforcement, first responders, those are the only ones who should need these types of bags. Not our kids!

Yet, here's a comparison no one is talking about. The U.S. Department of Defense reported 13 U.S. military personnel died due to hostile action (enemy attacks) in 2021.[11] In the school year ending in 2021, there were 43 school shootings with deaths, 50 school shootings with injuries only, and 53 reported school shootings with no casualties.[12]

There is a gauntlet of dangers kids must navigate through 13+ years of school. Is it any wonder teen suicide, anxiety, and depression are at historic highs?

It begs the question: is it safer to serve in the U.S. military or attend a traditional school in America?

This is not a pro-gun or anti-gun debate. This conversation must go beyond simply the weapon of choice and get to the root of the motivation. Why would so many former or current students direct such harm toward others in this system?

What are the root causes fueling this violence?

I would be doing you a great disservice if I didn't mention gun violence is *"only"* one of the life-threatening dangers kids face in traditional schools every single day. There is a gauntlet of dangers that kids must navigate through their 13+ years of school. We're talking bullying, suicide, self-harm, peer pressure, racism, substance and prescription addiction, academic and peer-oriented stress, and sleep deprivation, just to name the more prevalent ones. Is it any wonder why teen suicide rates and clinically diagnosable levels of anxiety and depression are at historic highs?[13]

I vividly remember routinely having sessions in our learning center with kids far into the night, and it was not uncommon to pull near-all-nighters. All this, as I already addressed, after seven hours of school, two to three more in extracurricular activities and sports, showing up with dinner in hand. For many of our students and their parents, late at night was the first and only time they got to connect that day. We saw firsthand what this grueling schedule was doing to kids. Our weekend break was typically Friday night through Saturday evening. But from the moment we opened Sunday morning, our tutors and specialists were meeting with students. And our study rooms were packed with students of all grade levels, cramming for the next test, or scrambling to write a paper before Monday.

And for what? For that all-important grade, of course. For a test, a paper, some high mark of supposed achievement, all sacrificing that child's sanity, childhood, sense of self-worth, and health in every area, for the next letter grade. I can't get out of my memory how many students suffered from exhaustion, stress, and panic attacks, many of them breaking down from the sheer pressure of the assignments and deadlines.

After almost every session, part of our communication with a student's parents included an itemized list of undone tasks for that student specific to just that session. Even after going home, many kids still had much to do before they were ready for school the next day. By the time students reached middle school in our area, they were carrying at least two to three hours of homework *every night*. It was even more for those who struggled.

When I taught seventh-grade history, literature, and English, I was told by the school how much homework to give. It created a double-edged sword because parents were constantly complaining about the homework load. And yet, it was those same parents who had high expectations on the amount of material they wanted the school to cover and to "make sure" their kids were learning all they "needed to."

More material, more material, and . . . more material. Guess what suffers the most when you pile hours and hours of homework (with the added pressure to make better grades) on a child? Their health. Both physical and mental.

A Stanford University study shows that students averaging over two hours of homework per night are more prone to suffer from sleep deprivation, weight loss, stomach problems, and headaches.[14]

> *"But, Christy, homework is good! Children need homework to score better on tests and do well in school!"*

This is what I thought too when I was a teacher. It was the only way to cover everything I was "supposed to." But studies at both Duke University and University of Virginia found that though homework can improve scores on standardized tests, it does not produce a measurable difference in school grades.[15] If our kids are suffering with more homework that doesn't truly improve their grades, then who benefits from homework? Let that sink in for a second . . .

A mom in our membership group shared with me the physical changes her daughter Kristin experienced after exiting the traditional school system for homeschooling. Kristin's stomach stopped hurting, she regained healthy eating habits, her skin tone looked much healthier, and her headaches went away in less than six months. The difference? Kristin was able to do all the schooling she needed in only a few hours a day with no homework at night. But all those health changes are just a coincidence, right?

One of the greatest cases in support of homeschooling over traditional schooling is the length and quality of sleep. National Jewish Health (NJH) conducted a recent study revealing that homeschooled students tend to be happier, physically and mentally healthier, and excelled academically and socially compared to traditional schooled students due to one key factor: sleep.[16] Homeschooled children tend to get more sleep and at a better quality than children who attend traditional schools.

The Center for Applied Research and Educational Improvement (CAREI) study published by the National Institute of Health (NIH) found that "Teens who are sleep-deprived or functioning with a sleep debt are shown to be more likely to experience symptoms such as depression, difficulty relating to peers and parents, and are more likely to use alcohol and other drugs."[17] What does the traditional school system push? Early start times, later nights with homework loads, and, from my 20+ years of educational experience, more time on the weekends preparing for tests and papers. The result? Sleep deprivation, lower quality of physical health, and myriad negative health effects.

The number of psychiatry visits related to self-harm and suicidal consideration more than doubles when school is in session.

The U.S. Department of Education discovered that the No. 1 reason why parents choose to homeschool their children is a concern about their school environment, such as safety, drugs, or negative peer pressure.[18] Yes, the U.S. government just said the quiet part aloud: parents want their kids to be safe, and they know kids who do school at home are healthier and safer.

As staggering as these physical health risks and dangers are to kids in traditional schools, it still pales in comparison to the systemic toxicity of mental health challenges from the school system.

Traditional Schooling Is Wreaking Unfathomable Damage on the Mental Health of Children and Teens

At our center, it was common practice for students to arrive in a state of overwhelm. I witnessed the multitude of stressors affecting students of every age. Academic challenges were just one part of the equation; the social pressures they faced added another layer of complexity. The demanding coursework, relentless assignments, and constant pursuit of success created an immense burden for these young individuals. But it didn't stop there.

The social dynamics at school also contributed to our students' stress. The need to fit in, the fear of judgment, and the pressure to navigate the complexities of peer relationships added an additional weight on their shoulders. It saddened me to see the toll it took on their mental well-being.

Now, I'm not a medical or mental health professional, but I can tell you several of the kids who came through our learning center over the course of our 17 years with ADHD were underdiagnosed or misdiagnosed. One mom swore her son James suffered with it, which is why he was in tutoring. But he didn't.

"Christy, you just said you're not a medical professional. How could you possibly know he didn't have this disability?"

I knew because James was retested by one of the best educational psychologists in the area and they made this discovery: James *never* had ADHD. James had an anxiety disorder,

Teenagers are the most stressed, anxious people in America, with 83% citing school as a cause.

heavily activated by the pressures of school. With the right diagnosis, intervention, and meds (this is a whole other can of worms), James was a completely different student: making great grades, doing well in school, and a much happier, more confident kid. I still wonder how much happier and healthier James would be in so many areas if he had the gift of homeschooling.

The reality is children and teens who are trapped in the traditional school system are in grave danger of suffering from mental health challenges. Here's a quick rundown of what the traditional school system is inflicting on our kids:

- **Suicide.** This is the third-leading killer of school-aged children ages 10 and older and the second-leading for ages 15 and older.[19]

- **Meds.** The number of psychiatry visits related to self-harm and suicidal consideration more than doubles when school is in session.[20]

- **Stress.** Teenagers are the most stressed, anxious people in America, with 83% citing school as a cause. Over one in four experience "extreme stress" during the school year compared to half that amount during the summer.[21]

- **Depression.** More than 4 in 10 school-aged students felt persistently sad or hopeless. Nearly one-third experienced poor mental health.[22]

Tragically, children and teens are at a much higher risk of developing mental health problems today than even 10 years ago.[23] It's vital we are vigilant about the various risk factors that children face at school. These encompass unhealthy peer-driven influences, excessive academic expectations, the rigidity of traditional classroom settings, negative social media trends amplified by peer-centered school culture, and the constant need to confront real physical danger.

We need to find the courage to call these out for what they are—accelerants to the mental health wildfire threatening our kids.

The good news is students who make the transition to homeschooling are seeing significant improvement in mental health. A 2021 Harvard study concluded that students who were homeschooled experienced more "well-being" than those attending public or private schools.[24] And several studies have shown that conventional schooling gives a "steady downward trend of self-concept as the child meets the pressures of the early school years."[25]

Why is that? Simply put, children and teens who home school are not as prone to peer orientation. There is a natural family structure where a loving adult can provide the perspective and support children of all ages desperately crave and need. But, what about the kids who graduate from homeschool and enter the "real world" of college? Are they truly prepared to be that much more well adjusted and emotionally healthy compared to their peers?

Saddle up.

Education researchers Drenovsky and Cohen found that, while levels of self-esteem didn't significantly differ, homeschooled students have lower depression scores, greater academic success, and rate their entire educational experience more positively.[26]

Homeschooled students have lower depression scores, greater academic success, and rate their entire educational experience more positively.

This begs the question: What makes the homeschool experience so different that kids view education and learning in a more positive light?

Our children cannot be expected to learn and live well when carrying so much stress and pressure. It's unrealistic to expect your child to be at their best when they're constantly worried about the next comment, incident, looming deadline, or insecurity that is stealing their joy. This is hard enough for adults, let alone kids whose brains are not fully developed yet.

This is why I use the analogy of homeschooling not being "sheltering" but a greenhouse protecting young plants as they mature, before they are ready to be on their own in the real world. And by "protecting" I mean being exposed to just enough (healthy stressors) but not too much (trauma) in their childhoods so they can become strong, resilient adult human beings.

It's not just homeschooling parents who see children being exposed to way too much far too early. In his book *Simplicity Parenting*, Kim John Payne highlights the importance of recognizing children are not developmentally prepared to handle the overwhelming burden of the adult world. According to Payne, modern society imposes adult-like expectations on children, which deprives them of a healthy and balanced childhood.[27] He advocates for simplifying children's lives by reducing excessive stimuli, schedules, and pressures. Payne emphasizes the significance of creating a nurturing and protected environment that respects children's natural developmental needs.[28]

While Payne stresses the need to simplify children's lives and protect them from overwhelming adult burdens, he does not dismiss the importance of preparing children for the realities of the world. Payne encourages finding a balance and gradually exposing children to age-appropriate challenges.[29] This is the perspective of almost every homeschool mom I know.

Homeschool is not "sheltering" but a greenhouse building strong, resilient adults.

If you know your child is struggling, or think it's even a possibility your child is facing or might face a mental health challenge, homeschooling may be the best decision to protect your child's health for the future.

Yes, Homeschooled Students Outpace Their Traditional School Peers in Academic Proficiency

Now, we're going to cover academic myths about home schooling in detail later, but let's dip our toes into this for a hot minute. You want your child to do well beyond graduation. So, how does homeschooling measure up academically against traditional schooling? Is homeschooling truly a better way for your child to get a good education? Will they be able to get into the schools they want to after high school, pursue the skill they want to develop, or create a thriving business?

First, let's take a real look at how U.S. public school students are doing with academics in the 2022 school year. Schools are academically failing our kids and the data might surprise you:

Public schools are failing our kids, with one in three falling below even the lowest reading or math level.

- 82% (est.) do not meet federal education standards.[30]
- 37% failed to meet their proficiency goals.[31]
- 19% of high school graduates cannot read.[32]

The National Assessment of Educational Progress (NAEP) *Basic* level of achievement is the least stringent measure of academic performance set by the National Assessment Governing Board. The number of public school students surveyed that scored below this level:[33]

- 25% of fourth graders scored below Basic level in math.
- 38% of eighth graders scored below Basic level in math.
- 37% of fourth graders scored below Basic level in reading.
- 30% of eighth graders scored below Basic level in reading.

And in each case, the number of students scoring below *Basic* level was greater than the year before. By state and jurisdiction,[34]

- Fourth-grade math scores declined in 43 states and juris- dictions and did not change in 10.
- Eighth-grade math scores declined in 51 and remained unchanged in two.
- Fourth-grade reading scores declined in 30 and were unchanged in 22.
- Eighth-grade reading scores declined in 33, did not change in 18, and rose in one.

Okay, so how do homeschoolers, as a group, compare academically? They excel.

- **Literacy.** Reading achievement tends to be a non-issue for most homeschool students, and reading achieve- ment scores are consistently higher than public school peers.[35] (Personal note: I've never met a homeschooled graduate who couldn't read.)

- **Standardized tests**. They also score 15 to 25 percentile points higher on average on standardized achievement tests (65 to 75 percentile compared to 50).[36] Black homeschool students score 23 to 42 percentile points higher than their black public-school counterparts.[37]

- **College admission tests.** Homeschooled students typically score above average on the SAT and ACT exams that colleges consider for admissions.[38]

- **College performance.** 78% of college surveyed admission officers said they expect homeschool graduates to perform as well as, or better than, traditional high school graduates.[39] Homeschool graduates are increasingly being actively recruited by colleges.[40]

- **College graduation rate.** Homeschooled students are nearly 10% more likely to graduate from college, with a graduation rate of 66.7%.[41]

Why is there such a significant difference in academic proficiency between traditionally schooled students and homeschooled students? For one, there are many academic benefits homeschoolers enjoy that kids in the system do not, including:

- Individualized instruction
- Flexible curriculum
- One-on-one attention
- Reduced distractions
- More efficient use of time
- Tailored pace of learning
- Individualized support for special needs

- Learning becoming the culture at home
- Phonics-based reading instruction from the start

The last one is a biggie for me. Homeschoolers have never really embraced the trendier approaches to teaching reading that popped up over the last 30 years. Traditionally schooled kids are consistently the subject of experimentation for whatever educational trends are in vogue. That brings me to this Public Service Announcement:

If your child was subjected to the catastrophic, albeit trendy, failure of the whole-language approach[42] to teaching literacy, this could be why your child struggles with reading.

Be on the lookout to avoid any reading program that leans primarily on sight words, and uses phrases like cueing, balanced literacy, and whole language.

> *Avoid any reading program that leans primarily on sight words, "cueing," "balanced literacy" and "whole language."*

During my teaching days, I distinctly remember the overwhelming sense that the students in my classroom weren't receiving the individual attention they truly deserved. There just wasn't sufficient time, energy, or resources to provide my students with the academic support they required to be at their personal best emotionally and academically.

Families and Relationships Are Suffering because of Traditional Schooling

We, as a society, have lost the understanding of what quality family time truly means. For so many parents, they are no longer the leaders and nurturers of their children. As soon as dinner is over, parents switch to being the "bad guy": "Alright, upstairs. Go do your homework." If that sounds painfully familiar, it means the traditional school system has enslaved you to be their enforcer at no extra pay and often at the excruciating cost of your relationship with your child.

This transfer of responsibility is shredding the precious fabric of parent-child bonds around the world, not just in the United States. And the worst part? Families aren't realizing how much of a relational deficit they're in because of this system-enforced servitude. When do families most realize there's a deficit? When they take a good vacation.

Think about your last vacation as a family. You had fun, right? You stayed up later. No homework, no school schedule, no stress from grades and papers on the horizon. You connected. You made amazing memories. And if it's been too long since your family had that type of connect time, why is that?

Because parents are now homework enforcers, conscripted into action by the school system, many not questioning if this is what they want as a parent.

A couple of years ago, I had the opportunity to attend a mid-summertime ladies' event, and I happened to be the only homeschool mom in the bunch. I vividly remember one mom sharing her vacation story, "Our family just needed it so bad. We desperately needed to reconnect." While I was happy to hear that time together was special for them, at the same time, I felt a deep ache in my heart.

Why are families satisfied with pent-up disconnect for the majority of the year, at the mercy of the school schedule?

Why are families satisfied with pent-up disconnect for the majority of the year, at the mercy of the school schedule that dictates when they will be given a window of reprieve to do something about it?

This arrangement is killing the joy of countless families. It's partly why 55% of Americans are dissatisfied with U.S. K–12 education.[43] The other reasons? Child safety, lack of academic proficiency, mental health challenges from a host of negative influences, and families feeling torn apart.

But I want you to have hope.

It's not too late for you and your child to stay connected. Or even reconnect.

Jessica's personal experience highlights the profound impact homeschooling can have on nurturing a renewed family bond. She shared with me how her son's affectionate nature faded away with each passing year in the traditional public school system.

However, since embarking on their homeschooling journey, Jessica is delighted by a heartwarming transformation. Randomly throughout the day, her three children now approach her with genuine hugs and conversation, creating beautiful moments of connection. Witnessing her 10-year-old son rediscover the joy of warm embraces fills Jessica's heart with deep appreciation. Her story showcases how homeschooling can rekindle the precious family bond that may be diminishing in conventional educational settings.

Homeschooling is not a magic elixir for family bonding. What it does create is a natural opportunity and the *time* for your family to stay connected and create more of those magical moments. The memories. The conversations. The experiences. The talks. Imagine having that amazing connection you feel on those great family vacations *every single day*. It doesn't have to be a pipe dream—it can become your new reality when you escape the control and limitations of the traditional school system and become the parent you want to be for your child every single day.

Will there still be times when you need to strongly encourage your child to do their schoolwork when homeschooling? For sure. Will there be days when you are banging your head against the wall in frustration? Of course! Homeschooling isn't pie in the sky. It's hard work. But most things worthy of doing aren't easy.

When you homeschool, you have the opportunity to design the atmosphere of your home and schooling. More importantly, it puts you in the driver's seat—not the passenger's seat—allowing you to choose how you want to grow, parent, and connect with your child.

Homeschooling creates more opportunity and time for your family to create those magical moments.

Homeschooled Students Are More Positive and Well Adjusted Compared to Traditionally Educated Students

Homeschooling gives you the freedom to discover what your child loves to learn. Is it possible that homeschooled kids can truly be happier and regain their love of learning with more freedom to pursue their interests and talents? Harvard seems to think so!

The Harvard University study referred to earlier found that homeschooled children not only experience more "well-being" compared to their public school-educated peers, but are also more likely to volunteer, be forgiving of others, develop a greater sense of purpose, and engage in healthier behaviors in their community.[44]

The school system's emphasis on memorization, regurgitation, testing, and grades suppresses intrinsic motivation and love for learning.

Let's stay in the Ivy League for a second (after all, aren't they the most revered educational institutions in the world?). How about their rival, Yale? A survey of 21,678 U.S. high school students by the Yale Center for Emotional Intelligence and the Yale Child Study Center found that nearly 75% of the students' self-reported feelings toward school were negative.[45]

The traditional school system is squelching children's natural thirst for learning because school feels like drudgery. Why is that the case? Because a vast majority of schools I've engaged with over 20+ years subscribe to a pedagogy (teaching methods and principles) in direct opposition to what we know ignites a love for learning and intrinsic motivation.[46] The traditional school system continues to maintain an emphasis on memorization, regurgitation, testing, and grades that shifts the focus away from that intrinsic motivation. Much of it can lack relevance, which causes disconnect and disinterest.

Pair that with the limited voice and choice students have in the classroom (they are told what to do, when to do it, and how), and you've got a formula guaranteed to make any normal child feel like school is the "bane of their existence." And we wonder why so many kids can't wait to get out of school each day. Remember staring at that school clock? It was so slow!

Homeschooling gives you the freedom to choose which pedagogy best fits your child's exact needs. You can empower your child to learn and mature at their own speed, with the freedom to do so without comparison to peers or a school pressuring them (or pressuring you) that they are "behind." A study published in the *Peabody Journal of Education* surveyed over 7,000 adults who were homeschooled as children and found that homeschooling had a positive impact on their personal and social development, as well as their academic achievement. The study also found that homeschooling was associated with greater independence, self-direction, and civic engagement in adulthood.[47]

Homeschooling is more than a valid educational alternative for families. It is the best way to provide tailored academics, instill a love for learning, foster greater social/emotional health, and curate more connected families. What many families *think* school is, and what it *truly* is, are two entirely different worlds. This became more apparent than ever when the entire world was sent home for Covid.

Remember staring at that school clock? It was so slow!

Homeschooling Changes the Conversation for Parents and Children

During the Covid-19 pandemic, millions of children were told to stay home while parents (maybe even yourself) scrambled to figure out "how to do school." To be fair to the many committed homeschoolers, this was not actual homeschooling. It was crisis schooling.

Although parents were suddenly handed the hot mess of trying to educate the kids of our nation, it also served as a profound eye-opener. Some realizations I've heard on repeat are:

- School can be done in less time when there isn't as much busy work.
- A lot of learning can be done independently.
- Seven hours a day is not required to complete the necessary coursework.
- Kids are receiving a poor quality education with a lot of useless information.
- Some course content is very disturbing to parents on both sides of the political aisle, and everywhere in between.
- Parents with kids who have special needs finding themselves able to provide their children a more tailored and supportive environment.

Homeschooling challenges traditional education, offering a refreshing alternative that puts individualized learning, flexibility, and personal freedom on center stage.

During the pandemic, people came to the realization that maybe, just maybe, homeschooling wasn't as challenging as they initially believed. Even though they were thrown into a crisis schooling situation, without the typical homeschooling setup, they started to see glimpses that homeschooling could truly be a solution to the frustrations they were experiencing with their kids in traditional schools.

Virtual schooling was underwhelming for so many parents that many simply decided to scrap it and go all-in with homeschooling during that time. The surge in homeschool curriculum sales further validates this point. I spoke to Jill from my Thrive Homeschool Community who told me that she was initially "forced" to homeschool due to the pandemic, but guess what? She ended up falling in love with all the benefits and is still going strong. It turned out completing the work was easier than anticipated, particularly when she took control of designing her own schooling instead of trying to enforce the school's coursework, which often complicates matters.

But it's not just the pandemic that ignited this conversation about education.

Dissatisfaction started stirring a long time ago. The pandemic simply served as a glaring spotlight, forcing us to confront what we already knew deep down but hadn't fully acknowledged.

Homeschooling shakes things up, challenging the traditional norms of education, offering a refreshing alternative that puts individualized learning, flexibility, and personal freedom on center stage. It opens the floodgates of discussion around personalized education, the crucial role of parents, and how education at home can foster a genuine love for learning.

Homeschooling sparks lively conversations about diverse curriculum choices, socialization adventures, and the ever-evolving landscape of education in today's world. It invites us to dive into a broader dialogue, celebrating the unique needs of learners and uncovering the incredible perks of stepping off the beaten path of traditional schooling.

It's no wonder we're witnessing an unprecedented surge in the number of homeschoolers, the likes of which have never been seen before. Parents, maybe even yourself, have realized that our children's formative years are a precious, once-in-a-lifetime chance to be truly present with those we hold dearest to our hearts.

We cannot afford to ignore the systemic risks and gross negligence our kids experience every time we send them out the door to a traditional school.

Imagine you're stuck in a building, not able to leave, constantly under threat of being sexually, physically, and verbally abused, or even assaulted, every single day; risking death at a moment's notice and being told you must conform to the authority's standards or face severe punishment and isolation. Your personal property can be searched at a moment's notice without hesitation.

That's not the Department of Corrections. That's the traditional school system.

The stats tell us that children and teens are at greater risk of physical harm and more likely to die from gun violence in school than on-duty U.S. military personnel.

Psychologists, therapists, psychiatrists, counselors, and mental health experts tell us that children are twice as likely to consider suicide because of traditional school pressures compared to home-based learning.[48] This is the type of "socialization" that homeschooled children are not getting.

Children and teens tell us they're happier, healthier, sleeping better, more fulfilled, and have a more positive outlook on life when homeschooling.

Parents just like you are telling us how much more joyful, connected, and loving they feel when they get quality time together beyond just an occasional weeklong vacation.

Our children's formative years are a precious, once-in-a-lifetime chance to be truly present with those we hold dearest to our hearts.

Here's what I know to be true . . .

The system we've trusted for over 150 years is not working for families, and it is our grave responsibility to have the courage to challenge why that is.

Remember This

- Homeschoolers, on average, outperform conventionally schooled kids on standardized tests, SATs, ACTs, college grades, and college graduation rates.

- Your child is at greater risk of suffering physical, mental, and emotional harm when attending a traditional school compared to being homeschooled.

- Traditional schools wreak unfathomable damage to children's mental health. Suicide is the third-leading killer of school-aged children.

PART TWO

The Great
Experiment

CHAPTER THREE

In Plain Sight: The Juicy History and Enduring Legacy of Public Schooling

"According to Plato the two most important questions for society [are] who will teach the children and what is taught to them. That was true 2,500 years ago and it is still true today. Sadly, today there simply is no agreement on who teaches the children and nothing but confusion and wildly different positions on what should be taught.

Therein lies the greatest threat to children in our modern age."

—Thomas Hampson, Founder, Truth Alliance Foundation[1]

Most Americans view our traditional school system as *the* "measuring stick" for all things education. Even if we don't agree with the overall experience, we, as a society, seem to accept this system as the inevitable way forward. How did we buy into this deeply held belief? Because it hasn't always been this way.

Are you ready to learn a scandalous secret? State-sponsored compulsory education as we know it today didn't even exist until around the time of the Civil War. Shocking, I know! For 200 years of American history, from the mid-1600s to the mid-1800s, the traditional school system as we know it didn't even exist.

Many of America's renowned Founding Fathers were homeschooled and those who weren't thrived in a choice-rich schooling system. As pointed out in the last chapter, this environment created some of the world's greatest leaders and thinkers of its time.

This is a history-heavy chapter, and if the Broadway smash hit Hamilton *taught us anything, history doesn't have to be boring. Let's mix it up a bit, à la reality show style.*

A cursory glance at this current flock of politicians and leaders in Washington, D.C., our culture at large, and many of the celebrities we venerate, prove critical thinking and courageous leadership are in severe danger.

What changed?

What if we hopped into our Wayback Machine and tried to find out how we got to where we are right now with education? We can look at what the best education used to be and why it's not practiced in the traditional school system anymore.

Some of the characters we'll cover may be familiar to you, but there are a few revered characters who may turn out to be the real culprits. There is no intention here to make offense, only to pull back the shrouds and present the truth. Just be prepared to encounter some ideas that today, well . . . let's just say they can ignite passionate responses.

Spoiler alert: the history of compulsory education in America cannot be fully told without encountering the intertwining threads of socialism. But before you raise an eyebrow, remember that these philosophies were the trendy talk of the town in the 19th century. Back then, folks were just trying to make sense of the world, throwing ideas around like confetti (well, maybe that's a slight exaggeration), and just like us, unaware of what the future held. We have the gift of hindsight.

So, let's give these players a generous pinch of understanding and a dash of graciousness. We'll try our best to give the "benefit of the doubt" about the intentions of people we don't really know whilst still acknowledging the monumental consequences of their actions because they were pretty darn significant and can't be ignored. So, grab some popcorn, snuggle in, and let's hit play on the backstory of how we got where we are with education . . .

Episode 1: Colonial America—The Scandal of Independent Thinking

If your background is anything like mine, you likely grew up in a more traditional school system, maybe even attending public school yourself. That's our starting point, our first scene—a glimpse into today's typical classroom where all the little desks are neatly arranged in rows. The bell rings. Children hastily stream in from their short recess, elbowing their way through the hallway traffic to their age-designated classrooms. Here we have age segregation in action, an integral part of the educational landscape.

A young and energetic teacher takes a position at the front of the room, armed with a government-prescribed curriculum designed specifically for this grade level. From math to language arts, science to social studies, each subject follows a carefully crafted path intended to ensure a standardized learning experience for all students. Oh, look, an apple on the desk. Picturesque, right? This is the scene we all remember whether it was our school or another school we saw on TV somewhere.

Imagine that—a school doing the will of its people and families, not that of the government.

Our Wayback Machine warmed up, we hop all the way back to the beginning of education history in the early days of America. Thirteen ragtag colonies. Pre–Betsy Ross and pre–George Washington trying out his new hatchet on his father's cherry tree. What do we see?

Kids running all over the place. Hardly any schoolhouses in sight. Who's doing most, if not, all the teaching?

Parents. At home! What? No, that can't be. Parents who haven't been teachers aren't qualified to teach their kids, right? Don't you have to go to college or have your teaching degree to teach your kids at home? Who do these parents think they are, teaching kids without a system to follow? Oh, the scandal!

What if you wanted more education for your child than what they could receive at home? Grammar and secondary schools have been popping up throughout the colonies. Many are started by the colonial government but financed and controlled by local townspeople. Imagine that—a school that truly wants to compete to be the best academic institution, without bending and compromising to some agenda or ideology. Doing the will of its people and families, not that of the government.

A newspaper (you remember those!) blows down the street and lands at our feet. Face up, the page shows an advertisement for one of these advanced schools. It trumpets a wide variety of subjects with instruction in Latin, Greek, trigonometry, bookkeeping, science, and English. We both have the same lightbulb moment—that's classical education!

Where we're standing right now, surrounded by the scribbling of letters and the pedagogy of ancient wisdom, is in the same classical education stream that spawned America's founding fathers, many of its early presidents, and its greatest leaders.

Strolling through town, aside from games of marbles and hopscotch, we find several children seated on benches in front of a store, immersed in classical texts, their budding intellects alight with curiosity. Across the street, several eagerly listening to an elder relate his experience of colonial history. And in the background, the buzz of conversation as other children engage with people of varying ages and backgrounds. This is a community that values classical education and its role in building the minds of future thinkers and leaders. But the townspeople don't think of it as a "classical" education. To them, it's just "education."

This isn't a romanticized walk down memory lane— this is real history.

Independent schools are here to serve families in their area. Compulsory education has no place here in colonial America because Americans are well on their way to educating their own kids.

> *Education was considered the responsibility of the family and local community of families, not the government.*

Since the founding of America in the early 17th century, education has been considered the responsibility of the family and local community of families, not the government.

Even so, if we were to jump to the end of this, the 18th century, we would see many states having decreed free public schools to help educate all children, regardless of social standing, and further, by 1870, all states having them.[2,3]

Speaking of the end of the 18th century, that's where we're headed next, but across the pond . . . so hang on!

Episode 2: The European Industrial Revolution—Factories, Steam, and Schooling for All

A cloud of steam, a chorus of cheers and applause. The buckets of water churned upwards out of the mine where we stand. We're covered in coal dust, lanterns spotlighting the row of newly installed steam engines. The floodwaters are quickly receding down here as this invention of commercial steam engines clears the way.

Europe is awash in a new wave of inventions: steam engines, factories, chemical and mechanical manufacturing, and an arms race of advancements in the name of industry. It's July 6, 1799, and France just declared its intent to join the race to industrialize.[4] Belgium, Great Britain, Spain, and any other European country worth its salt here in the late 18th century is also optimizing for innovative growth.

The engines' rhythms ring off the rocks towering overhead. This is the anthem of progress, isn't it? But who are those faces peering out behind the rocks? Children, some as young as five years old, covered head to toe with midnight shades of the mining underworld. Why aren't they in school? Why are they down in this dangerous dungeon of all places?

They're working!

We overhear the foreman "matter-of-factly" explain that children of all ages are employed in not just the mines, but in factories too. There's work to be done! He says, "It's for the good of the country, don't you know?" There's also talk about schools being opened and required for everyone.

What compelled parents to send their kids to work in mines and factories?

Poverty and economic challenges ravage the entire continent. Europe is making the transition from being an agricultural-based economy into an industrialized economy, and child labor (read: cheap labor) was part of the solution. It put food on the table for families, and helped transform Europe's economy.

Now, newly emerging factories require a literate and skilled workforce. The solution? A basic education to middle and lower-class kids, with a focus on practical skills. Basic education in the 3Rs and vocational skills provides that workforce, and this industrialized society moves forward.

State-sponsored compulsory education is finding its roots in the shadows of factories, bolstered by the newspapers' squished column inches trumpeting the next great invention. More and *Compulsory public education for thee, but not for me.* more nations are recognizing compulsory education as the ticket to economic prosperity and security. Every child needs to learn how to read, write, and do arithmetic to keep pushing the economy forward.

Now standing outside the clouds of coal dust, we see a different world. Upper class and nobles are riding by with their children looking quite different from the ones in the mine. Tutors and private instructors continue championing a classical education for those with a future in political, business, military, and religious leadership. Public education for thee, but not for me.

I crouch down to the road we are on and, with a short branch, manage to scratch a semblance of an X on the uneven rock and dirt. "This marks the point in time of a major shift in education. We're witnessing the birth of the dual-track education system in Europe; one for upper class children, leading to a university education, and one for everyone else, ending at vocational training.[5] And, as a result of public education becoming more available, we're also standing at the point when the study of classical curriculum begins to decline."[6,7]

More and more children are getting access to education as state-sponsored public education gains popularity across Europe. Won't it be such a gift! This will benefit people of all economic classes . . . right?

Episode 3: From Prussia with Love (and an Agenda)

A wide, sweeping panoramic shot, looking like the Austrian Alps in early scenes of *The Sound of Music*. Where is this? Prussia, a country nestled between what's now Germany and Poland, way ahead of most of Europe in one key area.

It's not so obvious at first. Everything looks like you'd expect in 1807.

Buildings, clothing, and technology are all on par with other countries in Europe. The difference? Prussia is light years ahead of everywhere else on the road to building a nationwide centralized compulsory education system.

They're already implementing state-sponsored schooling for children ages 5 through 13. All the children in Prussia are getting an education. With almost machine-like precision, standardized curricula rolls out across the country for every grade, including kindergarten. Formal teacher training creates a production line of teachers filing their way into classrooms. Prussia is the envy of Europe—who wouldn't be impressed with this advanced and modernized education? The crowning achievement? The "Abitur," a national final exam to prove you learned exactly what you needed.[8] (In fact, the Abitur is still used today!)

Who's this system for? Look at the classroom—all middle to lower class, no well-to-do students here. The wealthy kids are in their manors and mansions with tutors and private educators, being classically educated.

Church bells ringing. A rider races into town. News from the battlefront: Napoleon has crushed the Prussian army. Devastation and chaos are ripping like wildfire across the countryside.

The scene fades to black. Fast forward six months. A council meeting of Prussian military generals, all shouting accusations and calls for swift and decisive reform. Who's to blame for the loss? Certainly not the arrogance of an overmatched Prussian army against arguably the greatest conqueror since Alexander the Great. An idea, a brilliant idea from a (. . . ahem . . .) purely objective standpoint: the real problem isn't being outmanned, outmaneuvered and out-classed. The real problem is a lack of uniformity among the soldiers. We can't expect them to behave as one unit unless they've been trained as such from a young age. And where better to start than the classroom?

The chess pieces start moving: we overhear Prussian leaders discuss how conformity of behavior and obedience must be driven into young people earlier in school or there will be no future for their people. We look around and see many heads nodding in agreement. Enter two notable fig-ures, Wilhelm von Humboldt and Johann Gottlieb Fichte.

Fichte is appointed to reform the Prussian education system and plays a key role in the *Prussian General Regu-lations for Education*. These reforms aimed to create a stan-dardized and centralized system of education that would suppress individuality in order to promote the ideals of the state and cultivate loyal citizens. There's no need for sol-diers with critical thinking or individual initiative—just obey your officers who do, from wealthier families.

We're just in time to catch Fichte beginning a speech (italics, mine):

> "The new education must consist essentially in this, that it com-pletely *destroys freedom of will* in the soil which it undertakes to cultivate, and produces on the contrary, strict necessity in the decisions of the will, the opposite being impossible. Such a will can henceforth be relied on with confidence and certainty."[9]

Von Humboldt assumes a position overseeing the Sec-tion for Culture and Education in the Prussian Ministry of the Interior[10] and scribes this newfound belief system into

Prussian law.[11] Six, count 'em, six core pieces make up this state-enforced script for conformity:

- Compulsory education for lower and middle classes, including kindergarten: check.
- Centralized control of schools and teacher training: check.
- National testing of all students of both genders: check.
- Teaching recognized as a profession: check.
- Standardized one-size-fits-all model for each grade: check.
- Suppressing individuality, initiative, and critical thinking with authoritarian focus on conformity, obedience, duty, and discipline: check.

The latter point, shrouding over every subject, school, and community: Prussians can't be trusted to think for themselves—that's why they lost the war. Discipline, conformity, and obedience to the state become the gold standard of student behavior.[12]

Prussian education was intentionally designed to suppress free will, individuality, initiative, and critical thinking, and promote authoritarian conformity and obedience.

What's that sound? That's the sound of the other shoe dropping. Guess what Prussia started experiencing because of its compulsory standardized education?

- A great reduction of individual learning, interests, and experimentation.
- Rationed (i.e., reduced) education for low and middle-classes, to benefit the wealthy and ruling classes.

- Teachers becoming professionalized, planting the seeds in parents' minds that they are not qualified to teach their children without formal training.

- Testing and grades create an environment of extrinsic rewards, moving the focus from joy of leaning material to working for a grade.

- Teachers now "teaching to the test" to get better evaluations. "If my students test better, I must be doing a good job."

- Critical thinking and individuality are suppressed. We'll tell you what to think. Again, that's why we lost the war!

- Age segregation—separating students into age groups. The traditional mixed-age (and mixed curriculum) classroom is too inefficient for large numbers with the designated curriculum.

The Prussian education model and its psychological methods that imposed this "groupthink" on young minds are not going unnoticed by other European nations' ruling classes. It is starting to find new homes across Europe, and for reasons and practices that I contend neither you nor I would choose for our children.

Arguably, the most infamous adoption of the Prussian compulsory educational system was by a newly birthed nationalist party called the National Socialist German Workers' Party. We know it better by its historic name Nazi Germany. That cold realization stops us dead in our tracks as we see this train steaming forward through the history pages of Europe.

Episode 4: The Mann Who Imported the Great Experiment to the United States

The air is alive with a symphony of sounds, a harmonious blend of voices, footsteps, and the occasional clang of horse-drawn carriages traversing the cobblestone streets. It's afternoon in a bustling town square, and the air is abuzz with the chatter of parents, each contemplating the best path for their little ones.

Here, back on our side of the Atlantic, the concept of education takes on a different hue. America is thriving and insulated under the blanket of the Constitution, Bill of Rights, freedom, and a burgeoning economy. Accrediting agencies, regulatory boards, and teacher certification requirements don't exist here. America in the 1830s is one of the most well-read societies the world has ever seen, boasting literacy that would leave even the most discerning educator in awe.[13]

Private schools, church schools, academies, seminaries, and dames' schools each hold a unique allure, catering to the diverse needs and aspirations of families. Then, there are the common schools, the seeds of what would later bloom into the public school system, woven into the very fabric of the community.

In this wondrous tableau, local communities assert their autonomy, choosing their own standards and teachers who embody their values, and handpicking the textbooks that

1830s America was one of the most well-read societies the world has ever seen, where communities choose teachers and textbooks that embodied their own values.

will shape young minds. A sense of ownership pervades the air, as parents and educators alike work together to craft an educational tapestry that reflects the needs and aspirations of their unique corner of the world.

Meanwhile, in this post-colonial culture, discussions and conversations begin to stir in a nearby tavern. Amid the lively ambiance, air filled with the sounds of clinking glasses, and the enticing aroma of rich spirits, "perfecting" the social structure of America is a rich theme. Murmurs of utopian philosophies of socialism and collectivism echo high billing. A figure stands out within the crowd. Who is this high-cheekboned, white-haired man, making animated argument for educational reform?

At only 41 years old, Horace Mann is one of the fastest-rising voices in the Massachusetts legislature, and soon-to-be author of one of the most influential pieces of education legislation in U.S. history.

America's thriving choice-rich education system of homeschooling, grammar schools, and secondary education has been growing a unique ecosystem of academic rigor. But another system of education has recently caught Mann's eye. The Prussian education system had steadily grown across Europe, and Mann has fallen head over heels, enamored with its uniformity, order, and efficiency.

A toast is raised among the cheers . . . "The Great Experiment". . . his opus. And he may have just found the tool, and the support, to make it a reality—despite the freedoms many families and small townships wish to retain, for the best education possible for their children.

Controlling the teachers means controlling the children's values and ideologies.

And as the first secretary of the new Massachusetts Board of Education, Mann is about to set the stage for its adoption in the United States. Following the example of Prussia, he establishes teacher training institutions called "Normal Schools" to mold (i.e., "control") aspiring educators to transmit desired content, values, and ideologies to students. As in Prussia, controlling the teachers means controlling the children.

The scene changes and we find ourselves swept up in that panoramic snow-covered mountain shot again. We're back in Prussia, this time in 1843, almost 40 years since Prussia's defeat by Napoleon.

A man steps out of a carriage at the schoolhouse; it's Horace Mann again, on a tour of education systems, especially Prussian. We overhear Mann's welcome . . . he's beaming from the headmaster's flattery—is it true Mann is being called the "Father of American Education"? He doesn't deny it. What does Mann hope to learn from Prussia?

One giant step ahead to 1844 and we're back in Massachusetts. Mann's Seventh Annual Report as Secretary of the Board of Education in Massachusetts lies on the table in front of us and a few connected phrases jump off the page:

> "Prussia . . . excellence of its schools . . . models for the imitation . . ."14

Some dissent with key concerns about his claim. Henry Barnard points out some of the strenuous objections, both in Europe and America, to the Prussian system:[15]

> ". . . producing a spirit of blind acquiescence to arbitrary power."

> ". . . adapted to enslave, and not to enfranchise, the human mind."

Mann dismisses these concerns and insists on bringing this centralized, standardized, age-segregated, obedience-focused and compulsory philosophy into Massachusetts' school system. The meeting adjourns in favor of Mann's eloquence and recommendations: America will see its first compulsory school system. The Great Experiment begins.

The effect turns into a wholesale change as we see the years fly by—Mann driving this practice across the nation, with more and more families questioning this new approach to education.[16] It's a radical change from the status quo and we watch as the educational choices available to families slowly evaporate in the name of this reformation. And as we pass 1852, Massachusetts has become the first U.S. state to officially institute compulsory education. Game on.

1852: the landmark year American families begin to lose control over what their children will learn.

Is this what the future of education will be like in America? Will this new system be better for society? How will history remember Mann and his American version of compulsory education?

Episode 5: Meet John Dewey, Father of Progressive Education

The year is 1929. A flurry of sound bites, all from the same voice:

"I believe that education is the fundamental method of social progress and reform."[17]

"The school must be a genuine form of active community life, instead of a place set apart in which to learn lessons."

"The moral trinity of the school [is] the demand for social intelligence, social power, and social interests."[18]

Who is the speaker? Meet John Dewey, father of "progressive" education, and socialist. Like Horace Mann, Dewey saw early childhood education as a tool to help advance his ideology.[19] Just as Horace Mann spent time in Prussia to learn the country's education methods, Dewey recently traveled to Joseph Stalin's communist Russia to observe its system, in particular, how Russia achieved mass obedience and conformity.[20] We're overlooking an ornate table on which several of Dewey's articles are being worked on, a gold filigree pen off to the side awaiting a refill of ink. Getting a closer look, the article in progress resonates with praises of the Bolshevik Revolution, the headship of one Joseph Stalin, and the level of uniformity and control over their schools.

Okay, we can see that Dewey is interested in socialism. That's a popular topic of discussion in this era, as it was in Mann's. But what does that have to do with changing the American school system?

It wouldn't have made a difference had not Dewey become a person with great influence in the American educational establishment. He argues strongly that children need to develop a more holistic, communal view of the world; that impressing on them the tenets of a socialistic society should be the prime focus of early education, not learning the 3Rs and their application.[21] Because Dewey's reading methods will become so imbedded in American education, this day marks a defining juncture in American education: imprinting on students not how to think, but rather what to think.

In Dewey's 1898 manifesto, "The Primary Education Fetich," he argued that the insistence on having children study English so early in their schooling was cultish and a fetish,[22] and discussed how to help transform America into a socialist paradise slowly by changing how children learn to read.[23]

> *"The plea for the predominance of learning to read in early school-life because of the great importance attaching to literature seems to me a perversion."*[24]

More simply, Dewey argues that teaching children to read so early is warped or twisted.

As referenced earlier, America is one of the most literate societies the world has ever seen. But that was about to change.

Like all our preceding educational reformers, Dewey wants to use early education not to provide students better tools for learning, but to advance a change in American society.

Look to the left of his desk. See that book on his shelf? It's a McGuffy Reader. Published in 1836, with four reading levels all built on phonetics, it was the most successful reader of its time. But Dewey has his eye on relieving children of the difficulty of learning phonetics.[25]

How successful were Dewey's experimental methods? They were untested, had no scientific backing, and prominent physicians and neurologists contend that they would confuse the brain, decrease literacy, and cause learning disorders. Less than a decade from now, research conducted by neurologist Dr. Samuel Orton will confirm these assertions.[26,27] But by then, as they say, the train will have left the station . . . literally, as Dewey campaigned his idea throughout the country.

Dewey got the attention of oil billionaire John D. Rockefeller, who funded Dewey's experimental "Lincoln School" at Columbia University, where he sent his four children. Per Orton's warnings, all four developed learning disabilities after being subjected to Dewey's methods.[28]

> By the 1930s, "what" to think begins to replace "how" to think.

We mark this one as a spectacular disaster for education. But, unfortunately for children, it's a great success for marketing. As we zip through the 1930s and 1940s, despite the experts' warnings, we see Dewey's methods and new "Dick and Jane" readers spread across the American landscape.

And McGuffy is nowhere to be seen.

Episode 6: Back to Present Day

Raising the clear plastic guard over a red button labeled "home" and in moments we're back to present day. As we exit the Wayback, there's a noise behind us, and . . . just a moment . . . well, there we go . . . we've got a short summary of our trip:

- Colonial America using a classical education, enjoying high literacy, and producing some of the greatest minds and thinkers of its age.

- Europe in its Industrial Age, bringing compulsory schooling for the working class; a basic and "dumbed-down" education compared to what the wealthy and ruling classes provide to their children, but it's a win-win. Middle and lower classes get at least a little education, and the upper class gets workers for their factories and soldiers for its armies.

- Prussia doubling down on compulsory age-segregated basic education, adding psych methods to suppress critical thinking, individuality, and initiative, to build more compliant and obedient workers and soldiers. Leaving critical thinking and initiative for their superior officers, from wealthier families with better educations.

- Horace Mann's "Great Experiment" bringing Prussian compulsory education into the middle and lower classes in Massachusetts, then America; including establishing teacher schools to standardize (read: control) what was taught. American families losing their choice as to what their children will learn.

- John Dewey, pushing on American children an unscientific and unproven learning method, implemented not to benefit the children, but to imprint on them what to think rather than how to think.

> *"But, Christy, what about all the other things that have happened to our educational system—the General Education Board, the U.S. Department sound bites, decline of proficiency, . . ."*

Yes, there is a lot more we could unearth, but we've seen the major players who got us to where we are. And where is that? Why are our school not providing the best education possible?

Because they were never designed to. And, neither do they want to. So . . . what can we conclude by what we've seen?

The school system provides an inferior education to what existed prior, targeting practical skills rather than intellect. It develops not leaders and thinkers, but obedient and compliant employees by suppressing critical thinking, individual initiative, and independence. Age segregation causes inferior socialization, and a "one size fits all" approach causes problems for anyone on either side of "average" on the bell curve. And finally, its curriculum is always changing, driven by the winds of political and social agenda of whoever happens to be in power.

We are not living in a failed experiment. We are living in a system that does exactly what it was designed to do.

As Episode 6 rolls toward the credits, we look over our current landscape of education. We see families slowly morphing their relationships into age-segregated activities. Parents living in fear and stress that their child will not learn x, y, and z as the government schools say they must, to succeed in life.

Elementary-aged children facing immense societal pressure to achieve that almighty grade. Pre-teens and teens experiencing more peer-oriented influence and unrealistic expectations to perform their best; many in fight-or-flight mode with historic spikes in suicide attempts, addiction, and trauma markers.

Where is the hope? Is it too late for the families, children, teens, educators, and true advocates of freedom and choice to right so many wrongs? Spoiler alert: there's a bright glow on the horizon.

We've seen what else is available. And we've seen that we can opt out.

Episode 7: Recovering from This "Great Experiment"

State of Wisconsin v. Yoder (1972). We're in the U.S. Supreme Court courtroom where the case of three defendants, all Amish fathers, argue that their decision not to enroll their children in a public or private school is a First Amendment right.[29] The State of Wisconsin stands to gain a tremendous victory if the court rules in its favor.

The official word comes down only moments later: The State of Wisconsin's compulsory school attendance law is ruled unconstitutional. Homeschooling now has a historic precedent and freedom to opt out of state-sponsored compulsory school attendance. We see a flurry of legal action across the country over the next 10 years leading up to 1983 and the founding of the Home School Legal Defense Association (HSLDA). By the early 1990s, homeschooling is legalized in all 50 U.S. states.

There's a bright glow on the horizon. We've seen what else is available. And we've seen that we can opt out.

We now see a clear path forward for families, children, teens, medical experts, mental health experts, legislators, and advocates. We see a future where homeschooling can be a viable alternative to the traditional school system, which is failing our children. And we hold great hope as we see that the agenda and motives of those who wish to remove this choice from America's families are losing their power.

A growing chorus of voices inside the education space now also sees the light. Today, teachers are becoming so disillusioned with the traditional school system that each year 1 out of 12 teachers leave their positions.[30] Many of these educators are becoming advocates for homeschooling, like I did, seeing such a stark difference between what we defended for years compared to the reality we see today.

There is even a movement to make education independent of the state, as is religion. The Alliance for the Separation of School and State argues that parents are responsible for educating their children; that it is not a legitimate function of government; that our children should not be subject to the whims of politicians.[31]

The government has little to no business educating our children—it's a position we've negotiated away over the past 150 years.

Government education is failing our children and families. And this raises some significant questions:

- What is the best education available?

- In all honesty, do I want this for my children, or am I satisfied with the system as it is?

- If the schools won't provide my child the best education, what can I do?

- What have my children and my family lost already, can it be regained, and if so, how?

The government has little to no business educating our children—it's a position we've negotiated away over the past 150 years.

You and I likely grew up in the school system; it's what we know and learned to trust. Most of us had no idea how this came to be. Most probably assume it was because of problems in education that needed to be addressed or issues that needed to be fixed. The truth is that compulsory education in America was not started to provide a better education for kids. It was instituted by politicians to create changes to our society, to control and restrict not just what was being taught, but also students' very thinking processes. To suppress individuality, initiative and critical thinking needed for leaders, and to produce obedient, conforming and duty-bound workers and employees.

There were some things we found interesting, but for the most part, we found ourselves forced to sit still for hours on end, age-segregated with 30 or so peers, studying lesson topics we didn't care about, and working even more afterward at home to compete for grades on exams out of fear of what our parents would see on a report card.

We assumed this was the natural order of education, the right thing to do. Its practices have become ingrained in our mindset, our worldview, and it's hard to envision anything better. As Yeonmi Park noted in her book:

> "It's not easy to give up a worldview that is built into your bones and imprinted on your brain like the sound of your own father's voice."[32]

But now, we question that mindset.

What if education can be something that sparks our interest in learning and growing? What if the type of learning that can happen outside of the school system better prepares us for life? What if our natural bent for learning means we don't need professional teachers? What if someone with only a general high school education has all they need to nurture their child's learning, even sending them off to an Ivy League school?

We've seen how choices of motivated individuals can impact those within their sphere of influence. Your choices matter and impact those within your sphere. On cue, our Wayback Machine jumps in the opposite direction; we're now five years into the future, looking at some printouts and handwritten letters, spread out across a dining room table, some in crayon. They're from children that have been impacted by your life.

What if the type of learning that can happen outside of the school system better prepares us for life?

Are they learning to be critical thinkers, or to obey and not question? Are they becoming individuals, or conforming to others' expectations? Are they learning the great lessons and ideas from world history, or ignorant of them? Are they developing a love for books and education or a disdain?

This is your legacy. The result of your choices and your influence. But unlike Rembrandt's depiction of Belshazzar, you will be writing this future, and not on a wall, but on the very hearts and minds of children. What will that future say?

Remember This

- Until the 19th century, education was the responsibility of the family, and Colonial America had the highest literacy rate in the world.

- Our education system was designed to suppress individuality, initiative, and critical thinking needed for leaders, and to produce obedient, conforming, and duty-bound workers and employees. This structure has not changed.

- The public school system was never designed to give your child the best education possible; its architects were motivated politically. If a high-quality education is what you want for a child, you must look elsewhere.

CHAPTER FOUR

From Helpful to Harmful: What Changed in Education and Why It Matters

"There is a time to admire the grace and persuasive power of an influential idea, and there is a time to fear its hold over us. The time to worry is when the idea is so widely shared that we no longer even notice it. When it is so deeply rooted that it feels to us like plain, common sense. At the point when objections are not answered anymore because they are no longer even raised, we are not in control. We do not have the idea—it has us."

—Alfie Kohn, *Punished by Rewards*[1]

The crowd surges toward the palace, necks straining to catch a glimpse of the grand procession. Regal banners and the finest decorations set the stage for a remarkable occasion that all have gathered to witness.

A hush of reverence falls over the crowd as anticipation peaks—here he comes! Thousands upon thousands lay eyes on the royal leader in full splendor. However, reverence soon gives way to shock, and an awkward silence morphs into a flurry of whispered conversations. The shocking revelation defies even the most outrageous expectations—the rumors are true!

Following the full regalia, the leader carries himself with an air of indifference. To him, who are these peasants to understand the weight of his decisions? As Shakespeare reminds us, "Uneasy lies the head that wears a crown."

Amid a subdued hum of whispers, inhibition prevails. The emperor's advisors, motivated by self-interest and a fear of dissent, tirelessly assert his wisdom and infallibility, skillfully constructing an intricate illusion around him. As he continues down the street, undeterred by the growing tension, the innocent voice of a child shatters the dam of conformity . . .

"He's naked!"

The emperor, in all his arrogance and folly, is truly without clothes in the sight of his entire kingdom. He knew he was exposed. Those in his circle of confidence knew the irrationality of his decision. From the moment he set foot outside that day, it was obvious to so many others—those who equally feared the wrath of non-conformity and social pressure—to fall in line.

Until someone who didn't know any better pointed out the emperor's absurdity. All it took was someone who refused to play along with this game of groupthink. Out of the mouths of babes . . .

There's relief in realizing you don't have to conform, that you still hold the keys to your intellectual freedom and discernment of thought. I found some of my own freedom through the influence of a man named John.

John Taylor Gatto is a former New York State Teacher of the Year. An exemplary educator, the type of teacher you would love to lead your school.

There's just one problem: the longer he taught, the more he saw the damage the traditional school system wreaked on children.

Gatto became disillusioned with the school system, made his escape, and became an advocate for out-of-the-box education. What he said after leaving will forever stay in my mind. In his book *Dumbing Us Down: The Hidden Curriculum of Compulsory Schooling,* Gatto wrote he no longer wanted to "hurt kids to make a living . . ."[2]

There's relief in realizing you don't have to conform, that you still hold the keys to your intellectual freedom and discernment of thought.

He argued the standardized curriculum in American schools—and much of the intent behind its defense—is intentionally designed to suppress creativity and critical thinking skills. That wasn't always the case though, right? If we were to examine education through the lens of earlier periods in history, it becomes evident that education was seen as a means to empower intellectual discernment.

What changed, and why does it matter? The answer lies in the bedrock of learning.

Did Schooling Kill Education?

Did you have to teach your child to learn? Likely not. My four children, like seemingly every other child, all seem to have a natural curiosity. From their first few months, we see them stretch their arms, turn their heads toward sounds, and of course, that first baby laugh when seeing your face. Oh, how I miss those precious baby moments!

Kids watch so much of what's going on around them. They try new things.

They figure it out. They possess a knack for imitation, even to the point of emulating Dad's hilarious dance performance when he discovers it's taco night. Then, there is the ubiquitous one-word question that we learn to accept as parents: "Why?"

We are natural learners, and it's that innate instinct toward learning that drives us to discover a greater world. When a child is genuinely interested in something, they will pursue it and learn everything they can about it. The joy and satisfaction that come from stretching and discovering spark the curiosity to learn and grow.

As adults, we're not any different in that regard. We pursue the hobbies, activities, and sports that fascinate us, and we derive that same joy and satisfaction from stretching, learning, and doing.

But between birth and adulthood, there is a systemic starvation of curiosity. Learning no longer holds the joy we crave nor the challenge we desperately need. What happened?

School happened.

Like many educators, I used to think "schooling" and "education" were synonymous. So does *the Merriam-Webster Dictionary*, but the American Psychology Association (APA) recognizes the key difference. According to the APA, *education* is the process of learning that enables individuals to achieve their full potential in society. Schooling, by contrast, is "the structured experience in educational institutions."[3]

Schooling is no more a definition of learning than asphyxiation is a welcome form of breathing—both choke the life out of our very existence as human beings. As Albert Einstein once said, "The only thing that interferes with my learning is my education."[4] Education does not equal school. Learning does not equal school. And yet, this is the bias so many families, educators, and other well-meaning caregivers continue believing at the cost of their children's wellness.

> *Schooling is no more a definition of learning than asphyxiation is a welcome form of breathing—both choke the life out of our very existence as human beings.*

Enter more wisdom from John Taylor Gatto:

> "The truth is that schools don't really teach anything except how to obey orders . . . the abstract logic of the institution overwhelms their individual contributions. Although teachers do care and do work very, very hard, the institution is psychopathic—it has no conscience. It rings a bell and the young man in the middle of writing a poem must close his notebook and move to different cell where he must memorize that humans and monkeys derive from a common ancestor."[5]

Can we pause for a moment here because we need to acknowledge the group that Gatto just mentioned? There are educators still stuck in the system who simply haven't seen the light nor taken the step yet to leave the system. As Blumenfeld and Newman remind us in their book *Crimes of the Educators: How Utopians Are Using Government Schools to Destroy America's Children*:

> ". . . [M]ost teachers are unaware that they are complicit in this evil conspiracy. They simply do what they are taught to do by their professors of education. Few become aware that their professors deceived them and prepared them to create failure.

Most of these teachers are as much victims of the system as the students they are teaching."

As an experienced educator myself, I have respect for any teacher who wholeheartedly believes their work is making the greatest impact. To borrow from the words of H. G. Wells, "We were making the future and hardly any of us troubled to think what future we were making. And here it is!"[6]

I believed the same, and let me be clear: there are many educators who are making a remarkable difference in the lives of children and teens in the traditional school system. Do I believe they mean well? Yes. Do I believe good can still be done inside an overwhelmingly inept system? Yes, to an extent. Do I also inherently believe great educators are limited, at best, in such a system? Without question. Where does that leave us?

It leaves us in a place where no one wins—heartfelt talented teachers with amazing gifts, bound up by regulations and red tape; parents exasperated by the administration; and kids enduring educational governance that has long abandoned the best of what education could deliver.

What if the traditional school system is not as adept at educating children as we've been told? What if we start rethinking the idea of schooling, that education is not the same as school?

The shift from learning to schooling is the most crucial for us to explore in this immediate context.

For many students, and even some educators, school is perceived as work to endure, not learning to enjoy, in no thanks to six serious changes.

Changing the Purpose of Education

Why did you bother with school? Was it to score that diploma, then chase after a degree just so you could land a job interview? And the whole time, you had to keep your transcript in check, hoping it would be "good enough" to impress potential employers. But here's the kicker: The criteria they use to evaluate your worth on the job might leave you scratching your head, wondering why those particular measures even matter.

Consider the countless hours you spent pouring over textbooks, attending lectures, and preparing for exams throughout your school years. It was all part of a journey aimed at achieving that coveted diploma, which was just the first milestone on your educational path. But then came the pursuit of a higher degree, with the hope that it would open doors to promising job opportunities.

Along the way, you meticulously maintained your academic transcript, striving for excellence, and constantly second-guessing whether it would impress future employers. Fast forward to job interviews where you find yourself grappling with perplexing assessment criteria. Interviewers may inquire about your ability to solve hypothetical problems, assess your capacity for adaptability and communication, pose questions aimed at gauging emotional maturity, or evaluate your proficiency in specific software tools. It's a perplexing journey from school to the job market, where the bridge between education and employment sometimes seems shrouded in mystery.

It's like the truly useless information you learned in school, which ate up a big chunk of your life, hardly aligned with the real-world knowledge and skills needed for your actual career. It's enough to make you question the whole system.

For many modern societies, including and maybe especially American society, it's normalized to treat education as a means to an end. School is a 13-year necessary evil to become an "adult," a contributing member of society as some would lead us to believe. Only 150 years ago, a mere blip in the timeline of humanity, education was not the means to the end—education was the end. During our whirlwind tour through history, if we'd asked someone in colonial America if they were a lifelong learner, they would have laughed. Of course they were lifelong learners—everyone was a lifelong learner in that time of history.

Today, however, we find ourselves in a different landscape. The emphasis on education as a stepping stone to a career has grown, and this shift has significant implications. It raises questions about the true purpose of education in the modern world. Are we nurturing lifelong learners who relish the pursuit of knowledge for its own sake, or are we churning out individuals who see education merely as a ticket to a paycheck? The current system often prioritizes rote memorization and standardized testing, which can discourage curiosity and critical thinking. The challenge lies in striking a balance between the practical skills needed for employment and the intrinsic value of knowledge for its own sake.

And yet, the traditional school system conditions our collective brains to believe learning is only essential until graduation. If anything must be learned after you graduate, it's viewed as an inconvenient bridge to the next promotion, job offer, or round of interviews. By changing the purpose of education, the traditional school system deprives children, teens, and eventual adults of learning because the target is off our original course.

How do we reclaim the intended purpose of education? How might we inspire our children, our families, and even ourselves to rekindle that spark of lifelong learning? By loving what is lovely, and learning what is worthy of our fleeting time in this life. To paraphrase Whitman,

> *Only 150 years ago, a mere blip in the timeline of humanity, education was not the means to the end— education was the end.*

> Of the recurring question, what is the good and beautiful purpose of life? That you are here—that life and identity exist, that the powerful play goes on, and you may contribute a verse.[7]

From the confines of a coercive education system, where children are stripped of agency and repeatedly instructed on what, when and where to learn, we suddenly expect them to confidently choose their lifelong pursuits when they reach the age of 18. How can we expect our children to select a career path (i.e., major), let alone possess the essential skills, knowledge and maturity for such a decision, after being conditioned by an educational system that controlled every aspect of their learning?

> *How can our children possess the skills, knowledge, and maturity to select a career path after being conditioned by an educational system that controlled every aspect of their learning?*

For 13 years straight, we suppressed their desires and taught them how to learn without any passion. Now, we suddenly want them to use an atrophied voice of opinion about what matters to them. What happened to those interests during that time?

Pursuing what is lovely requires time, and a seven-hour-plus school day is a death sentence for inspired thought. Where is the time to find and pursue what you love? For children and teens in the traditional school system, that time is tucked in the scraggly sparse minutes between classes, bleary-eyed and in fight-or-flight mode counting down the minutes until freedom. At best, they are treated with a mountain of homework, and at worst, wondering whether their day will end in tears, a panic attack, a drugged stupor, or worse. This cannot be the best way forward.

Our children deserve so much more. For countless families, homeschooling clears the canvas of creativity for children to explore and discover what ignites their souls and curiosity about learning. You get to rewrite the purpose of education with your child's best interests in mind. One of the many freedoms homeschooling gives is the ability to give your child classes that align with their interests. Whether it's this year or far down the road, you can co-create your child's transcript to show their interests in a remarkably different light.

Yes, your child can have an excellent education with your guidance, but it can have a greater purpose when you know they are free to pursue what is delightful to their minds.

Changing the Skills of Education

"So, how's school?" If your child has been in the traditional school system for any stretch of time, you'll likely hear something like this:

- "We had a test. I got a 97."

- "I'm failing AP Calc . . ."

- "Got an *A-* on my paper."

What's the central theme? It's better to regurgitate rote information instead of learning how to critically think. In fairness to many educators in the system, there is extraordinary pressure for teachers to "teach to the test." As we saw in the Prussian school system, teachers whose students did better on standardized tests were deemed "good teachers," so of course, (. . . ahem . . .) "they must be doing it right."

The system has not changed.

That was my story for years as a teacher-turned-learning center director. It was far more important to have students give the teacher exactly what they wanted for three reasons: (1) your perceived value as a student was far greater with an *A* next to your name, (2) your teacher was rewarded when you did "well," and (3) there simply wasn't enough time to learn things outside of the prescribed standards.

Students are snowed-in under an avalanche of homework, emotional and mental health pressure and challenges, and relational strain from

Homeschooling clears the canvas of creativity for children to explore and discover what ignites their souls and curiosity about learning.

parents who feel like strangers under the same roof. The easier, more celebrated route is to focus only on satisfying a teacher's personal views on the subject. Just give the teacher what they want to hear. End of story.

If critical thinking and learning for the sake of learning are no longer championed in the modern school system, then what skills are rewarded instead?

- Surviving at all costs in an academic setting.

- Faking competency just long enough to pass or graduate, whichever seems easiest at the time.

- "Working the system" in all sorts of ways that often have little to do with academic learning.

Writing papers more in line with a teacher's personal beliefs, memorizing study guides, or getting extra credit for attending the boys' basketball game on Friday can change that C+ to a solid B.

What does it take to truly embrace the potential of learning without the easy outs of a study guide, passing grades, or faking competency? The road less traveled is called critical thinking. What's the reward? That you are developing a mind so potent in engaging thought that it is prepared for any topic, conversation, or opportunity.

> *What's the reward? That you are developing a mind so potent in engaging thought that it is prepared for any topic, conversation, or opportunity.*

It's why I see so many homeschoolers stand head and shoulders above their traditional school counterparts in the areas of debate, engaging dialogue, critical thinking exams, including the SAT and ACT, and navigating complex gray areas of ideology. The skills of our Founding Fathers that carved the canal of the Constitution in the gray matter of colonial America are the same skills that can reclaim our freedoms of intellectual thought today.

Those are skills worth strengthening in your child for life.

Changing the Focus of Education

How do you know someone is a good student *without* using grades as any metric of competency? You would be amazed at how this simple question stumps even seasoned educators. Can I share the real reason? It's because grades are the Holy Grail of academic success. Good grades equal being a good student, which obviously means they have a good teacher who is obviously led by a good administrator and unwavering proof that this is a good school. Take away the letter grades though, and how would you know who's a good student?

A damning change in the traditional school system, is that the focus switched from learning for the sake of competency, to schooling for the sake of grades. The definition of success in school shifted into a letter-driven standard by which *all* students are equally, yet unfairly, judged. And yet, the accepted way to evaluate hundreds of kids in a traditional school setting is with testing and grades. While well intended, this approach completely falls short as an effective way to evaluate. A more genuine way to assess a child's learning is to engage in thoughtful conversations.

> *A more genuine way to assess a child's learning is to engage in thoughtful conversations.*

What does this letter-grade system spell for our future? That obedience without question is the ultimate watermark of a poster-child student. Conforming to the system, assuming the beliefs and values of your teachers (for fear of failure), and modifying your behavior to be more agreeable as a student, are all rewarded. That's what's being learned in the school system today.

A grade-centric schooling process allows students to achieve great grades without truly obtaining an education. This is compounded by the intense pressure on teachers, who face constant changes in standards and round-the-clock scrutiny of student progress by parents. Parents don't want Cs. Cs have become the new Fs. While the system suggests that education is quantified by grades, true education is better assessed by our mastery of critical concepts and thoughtful analysis

> *"But, Christy, I don't want my child to struggle! They need good grades to get into college!"*

I hear you, and you're right—grades matter to colleges that are looking for the right type of students. That said, if your child struggles in a class, works hard, and still gets a C+, are you still proud of their work? What if they work harder in that class than they've ever worked in any other class, and their grade is still far below an A, are you still going to celebrate their effort?

In the journey toward a college degree, maintaining good grades is undoubtedly essential, as it opens doors to higher education institutions and job prospects. However, it's equally crucial to acknowledge that not all students have the same academic strengths or circumstances. Some may face challenges that affect their grades, but they could still be hardworking, creative, and innovative individuals who possess valuable skills beyond what a transcript might reveal.

Therefore, it's worth considering a broader perspective that goes beyond grades and values qualities like determination, problem-solving abilities, and integrity. Such a perspective challenges the existing system's emphasis on grades as the sole measure of one's potential.

And, yet, how essential is that college degree in this age? For pursuing one's passion in advanced knowledge-based areas, yes. But remember that school, including advanced education, builds obedient followers, not resourceful leaders. It is those intangible skills, beyond what a transcript might reveal, that bring success. We have superseded the industrial era with online tools that level the entryway for creatives and innovators. No longer are we surprised to hear of growing careers and businesses birthed out of bedrooms, garages, or kitchens. Do you own a smartphone? Then you have the tools to write, publish, create, record, buy, sell, bill and collect; and yes, to hire those college graduates to come and work for *you*.

It is those intangible skills, beyond what a transcript might reveal, that bring success.

But more importantly, let me arm you with this truth to stand on. A grade-centric system often favors a specific type of student, leaving little room for the unique and innovative learners who don't fit in the box.

Do you or someone you know own an Apple iPhone? Maybe an iPad?

Maybe . . . a personal computer or a music player of any brand? Apple co-founder and CEO Steve Jobs was the driving force that brought these innovations to market.[8] He revolutionized how we communicate, listen to music, and share information. And he was one of these people whose genius couldn't be measured by grades. His combination of practical engineering with a profound aesthetic sensibility[9] drove his Apple engineers nuts, as he repeatedly rejected designs that did not meet his discriminating sense.

Yet Jobs didn't graduate from college. After a semester at Reed College, only intermittently attending required classes that didn't interest him, he dropped out. He then spent the following 18 months there auditing classes in the arts that did interest him—dirt poor, barefoot, and sleeping on the floor in friends' dorm rooms.[10]

By placing exclusive emphasis on grades, we may unintentionally neglect the diverse talents and potential of many children. This mentality is deeply ingrained in us over the course of 13 years of formal education and can be challenging, if not impossible, to undo on evenings and weekends. However, as dedicated homeschooling parents, you have the power to reshape this narrative and nurture your children's confidence in their multifaceted abilities and strengths.

Embrace the journey of holistic learning and know that you're equipping them with the resilience and self-worth needed to thrive beyond the confines of conventional grading.

Changing the Motivation of Education

Think back to your own schooling. Preschool, college, grade school, high school—it largely doesn't matter *what* level of school it was. Why did you want to do well in school? To feel a sense of accomplishment? To have a higher sense of self-worth? To know you could perform to a certain level of achievement? To get a more esteemed degree? I will confess those were all reasons why I wanted to do well in school.

It's natural to draw some sense of our well-being from what we accomplish. Learning is an accomplishment, but what is the motivation to learn? For many students, the diploma or degree is the carrot at the end of the stick. The micro-rewards along the way are often good grades, receiving

We were never meant to learn only to achieve— we're meant to learn so we can embody an indelibly beautiful life.

honors and recognition, enrollment in more advanced classes, and a sparkling transcript built for your dream school to fall in love with you.

Schooling changed when more emphasis was placed on extrinsic motivators instead of the intrinsic reward of learning for the sake of learning. The passion for picking up a book rich with substantive thought was sacrificed on the altar of graduation. As the brilliant Peter Gray wrote:

> "We no longer use the cane, as schoolmasters once did, but instead rely on a system of incessant testing, grading, and ranking of children compared with their peers. We thereby tap into and distort the human emotional systems of shame and pride to motivate children to do the work. Children are made to feel ashamed if they perform worse than their peers and pride if they perform better."[11]

Confusing achievement for learning cheapens the role of education. We were never meant to learn only to achieve— we're meant to learn so we can embody an indelibly beautiful life. Achieving is not the only reward, and wrapping our self-worth in the cloak of accomplishments is damning to our innate value as human beings. The journey of learning on the road to achieving is equally rewarding.

Changing of the Guard for Education

G. K. Chesterton once said, "The only people who seem to have nothing to do with the education of the children are the parents."[12] When your child is at school, to whom do they belong? It depends on who you ask. Most parents I've met firmly believe they are the ones who are ultimately in control of their child's education.

Ask those in the educational establishment and you'll get a different answer altogether—one that is currently supported by the weight of U.S. federal court precedent.

Throughout history there's been a continuous battle for the minds of children. Those with agendas often seek educational governance over impressionable young minds, knowing that if they spend enough time influencing children, they can imprint them with ideas that might even oppose parental values.

Henry Barnard, a well-recognized champion of compulsory education in the United States (and whom we briefly met in Chapter 3) said the quiet part aloud:

> "No one at all familiar with the deficient household arrangements and deranged machinery of domestic life, of the extreme poor, and ignorant, to say nothing of the intemperate . . . can doubt, that it *is better for children to be removed as early and as long as possible* from such scenes and examples."[13]

Translation: Barnard believed that children should be removed from household influences, including their parents, as soon as possible. The 9th Circuit Court of Appeals sides with the state: parents give up their rights when their children enter public School grounds:[14]

> "In summary, we hold that there is no free-standing fundamental right of parents to control the upbringing of their children by introducing them to matters of and relating to sex in accordance with their personal and religious values and beliefs . . ."

And:

> "We conclude only that the parents are possessed of no constitutional right to prevent the public schools from providing information on that subject to their students in any forum or manner they select."

In other words, schools and educators alike believe they can do whatever they want, in any way they want, including bringing in whomever they want with unfettered access to your child. If such a power is monopolized by the government, the politically powerful will forever make such decisions.

As Arnold Toynbee so eloquently said,

> "Whoever controls the image and information of the past determines what and how future generations will think; whoever controls the information and the images of the present determines how those same people will view the past."[15]

The changing of the guard from parents being the trusted voices guiding their child's education to the state's claim to ownership is a devastating blow to critical thought. Even worse, it is a direct threat to independent freedoms.

The key issue at stake here is "parental rights." A wildly popular article by Harvard Law Professor Elizabeth Bartholet published in the *Arizona Law Review* trumpeted the claim that you as a parent, should you choose to homeschool, would see nothing wrong with having absolute control over your child's education, including neglecting to educate them.[16]

There are three clear fallacies Bartholet commits while painting with her "broad brush:"

1. Representing that isolated cases of child maltreatment by a few criminal parents accurately represents homeschoolers.

2. Attacking this exaggerated and distorted portrayal rather than addressing the true practices and motivations of homeschooling families.

3. Framing this issue as having only two choices: unrestricted "potentially criminal" homeschooling, or none; ignoring the wide range of other possibilities between.

Yes, I included the link in the endnotes if you'd rather read Bartholet's article in its entirety. A glass of wine will likely make the experience more palatable.

You wouldn't give any random person access to your bank account, but we're expected to simply hand over our children without question or restraint.

The Homeschool Legal Defense Association (HSLDA) produced a series of rebuttal articles to Bartholet's op-ed. HSLDA's series of responses focuses on a clear delineation between two sets of rights: absolute rights and fundamental rights.[17] Of the two, parental rights are fundamental in nature, and it is that right we must exercise out of love, wisdom, and protection for the children within our care.

As I stated earlier, you wouldn't give any random person access to your bank account, but we're expected to hand over our children without question. The inconvenient truth is that the philosophy of education in today's school system resembles very little of our Founding Fathers' intentions and more of the tyrannical agenda held by the very people our founders fought so hard to defeat.

And why is that the case? To quote John Taylor Gatto:

> "Schools were designed by Horace Mann and by Sears and Harper of the University of Chicago and by Thorndyke of Columbia Teachers College and by some other men to be instruments for the scientific management of the mass population. Schools are intended to produce, through the application of formulas, formulaic human beings whose behavior can be predicted and controlled."[18]

Alvin Toffler describes this behavior-control formula in one of the most influential books of the 20th century, *Future Shock*:

> The most criticized features of education today—the regimentation, lack of individualization, the rigid systems of seating, grouping, grading, and marking, the authoritarian role of the teacher—are precisely those that made mass public education so effective an instrument of adaptation.[19]

It is within your power to change the guard again for your child's education. Taking responsibility for your child to learn, grow, and understand key principles of education for their future is one of our most cherished gifts. That is an unquestionable right every parent must protect without fail.

Changing the Pedagogy of Education

A chalkboard at the front of the room, rows and rows of desks facing the front, and a lecture-style mathematics lesson. The setting is the same, but the era in which this classroom is set could be the 1860s or the 2020s. However, hidden beneath this visual continuity is a significant historical shift. About 150 years ago, a seismic transformation occurred in how we approached education, reshaping its very essence. This transformation lies in the pedagogy—the way we educate children.

This shift marked the emergence of the traditional school system, even though the classroom's appearance remained remarkably unchanged.

To truly understand the shift in the pedagogy of education, we need to revisit the very definition of *pedagogy*. A household name from the past, *Merriam-Webster's Dictionary*, can help us start with a base definition of this term:

Pedagogy, noun: the art, science, or profession of teaching.[20]

It's a broad enough term, to be sure, and that is where the deterioration of the school system finds much of its roots. Pedagogy in the modern era, what we've been referring to as the traditional school system, is now believed to be synonymous with an industrialized, age-segregated, and comparison and competition-heavy environment.

Contrast that with the rich learning environment of how education used to be done, often referred to as classical education, dating back to ancient Greece, Rome, and even earlier in history: focusing on mastery, nurturing wonder and curiosity, pursuing what is good, beautiful, and true; and resting your pace of life to have the capacity to consider new truths and turn complex conversations into learning experiences.

You hold the keys to reverse the decisions and influences that hijacked our society's understanding of "learning."

The modern, traditional school pedagogy thrives on regurgitation, standardized testing, an overwhelming amount of homework that serves little to no purpose, an age-segregated caste of academics, and authoritative instruction. Compare that to these eight principles of a true classical education based on love, beauty, wonder, curiosity, and other virtues.

Is there any reason to believe the traditional school system's pedagogy can even compare to classical education pedagogy?

These six changes show the stark contrast between the origins of education and the cold reality children, teens, and their families are suffering from in our current school system.

Can I share some good news? Change is still within your control. You hold the keys to your child's learning. You can reverse the decisions and influences that hijacked our society's understanding of education. If you'll dream with me for a bit longer, there is a lighted pathway out of this darkness.

It's the hope of realizing what's possible.

Remember This

- Education has shifted from seeking learning and mastery to seeking grades and avoiding public shame.

- The primary authority has also shifted, from resting with parents to now being controlled by the government.

- The rich learning experience of classical education has been replaced with an age-segregated competition-heavy model stressing compliance and conformity.

- You can go through 13 years of schooling and never receive an education.

PART THREE

The Extraordinary Potential of Homeschooling

CHAPTER FIVE

The Homeschooling Edge: Where Possibilities Flourish

"Give a child a single valuable idea, and you have done more for their education than if you had laid upon their mind the burden of bushels of information."

—Charlotte Mason

His frustration was palpable. "Mom, I don't know how to do this!"

It caught me off guard. Hadn't we tackled these math facts just a few months ago? My son wasn't typically one to stumble in mathematics, so this sudden roadblock was surprising. We had indeed covered the ground less than four months back, going over the material meticulously.

It was then that I recognized my mistake. Despite my background as a seasoned educator, I momentarily overlooked a fundamental truth. Learning, I knew all too well, is a nuanced journey. Yet, in this crucial moment, I stood at a crossroads: forge ahead with our existing curriculum, or hit pause, fortify our grasp on math facts, and then resume from where we had left off.

Together, despite not knowing how long it would take, and at the risk of "getting behind" in the math curriculum, we chose Option No. 2. We put our math curriculum on hold, dedicating the next three weeks to an intensive review of our math facts. This time, we delved even deeper.

After nearly a month, we picked up our math curriculum again. His progress was nothing short of remarkable. It was exactly what he needed. A poignant lesson stayed with me. It was a stark reminder that assuming a concept is 'mastered' after a single pass isn't realistic. While they might grasp it initially, my children, like all of us, are only human. We can learn something once, and then with time, find ourselves forgetting it and in need of a refresher.

Yet, it also served as a stark reminder of an unyielding truth. In a conventional school setting, my son wouldn't have had the luxury of hitting pause to review what he needed. He would have been tethered to extra hours, working with a tutor if that was in the budget, all the while, the math class charging ahead without him. Like so many kids in the school system, he'd be left to bridge a growing chasm, falling further and further behind.

The Power of Stopping, Slowing Down, or Speeding Up

That's where gaps, learning insecurities, and shaming yourself about where you are with school all start showing up. Those nasty, joy-stealing problems are keeping great kids from enjoying life to the fullest because the traditional school system is like a train. It runs on a fixed track at a fixed pace, not slowing down when someone needs it to. Students can pull on that brake cord all they want, but "the ol' train, she ain't slowin' down." Nor does it speed up for those who are insufficiently challenged and need more stimulation.

I wonder how many kids are truly still on the train when it reaches its end-of-the-year destination. And what happens to all the kids who were left behind with no means to catch up? Our learning center, full to the brim on a daily basis, stands as proof that many, many children are left on the side of the tracks at some point during the year.

You've seen what happens to a child's joy when they start failing in school, right? I saw this play out countless times over the course of my career. Students would hit a difficult concept or a new section in a particular class, often math, science, or writing, and kids who were normally joyful and loving life would show up with clouds hanging over their heads. It wasn't that the concept was the problem—it was *how* the pace of learning made them feel.

The traditional school system is like a train: running on a fixed track at a fixed pace, not slowing down when someone needs it to. With homeschooling, we can slow and even stop the train.

Like they were somehow not as smart as the rest of the class. Like they were "lesser than" because one new concept got the better of their brains in that moment. It's not their fault that trigonometry, calculus, and physics are tough subjects. You remember those classes. These kids are simply the victims of a system that moves at a set speed. If you want to go any faster or need to go slower, you hit a wall *hard*.

With homeschooling, we can stop the train.

I consulted with Robin a short while ago. "Christy, I'm going to be homeschooling my son. What curriculum do I need?" As with every parent who tells me they're going to homeschool and asks about curriculum, I wanted to know Robin's reason for homeschooling.

Her answer? Robin's eighth-grade son Tim was reading at a fourth-grade level. We didn't need to talk about curriculum—we needed to help Tim get support for his reading. He started working with a reading tutor and his reading is much better now. Tim's issues were never going to autocorrect; neither was the school system going to slow down the pace or provide help. They were content to just keep dragging him down the track behind the caboose to the next station, either hoping his problem would magically resolve itself or leaving it for next year's teacher to address.

Who suffers in this situation? Kids like Tim. The way the system is structured can lead to children developing negative and potentially toxic beliefs about themselves, depending on their individual learning differences and preferences. "Sorting" and grouping kids as the stragglers in their school dumps a load of mental shame on amazing children who are simply asynchronous learners—that is, learning different subjects at different speeds.

If we don't allow room for these varying paces, what are these kids going to start believing about themselves? "I'm too dumb . . ." "I'm not smart . . ." "I'm terrible at school . . ." Their learning pace is not the problem— the pace of teaching is. But in mass schooling, teachers have no choice.

Being able to stop, slow down, or speed up depending on what your child needs is *so* important. Otherwise, we're teaching our kids the speed of knowledge consumption matters more than the depth of comprehension.

In homeschool, we have the flexibility to take intentional pauses in education to strengthen our learning.

There is beauty in flexibility, especially when it comes to giving your child the freedom to learn at their own pace. If your child is devouring a subject at a voracious pace, why put a limit on how fast they can learn? I see homeschooled children reading at several grade levels above their age. There's also a fun little response when people ask homeschooled kids, "What grade are you?" and the kids respond, "What subject?" This idea of having grade-specific capabilities flies in the face of learning for one key reason.

We, as humans, are asynchronous learners. Our learning pace and development are uneven because there are so many moving parts of our physical development and psyche. If we all learned at the exact same pace with *every* subject or area of educational learning, we would be, what's the word . . . *industrialized* clones of finished products. Sound familiar?

It doesn't have to be this way. You can throw off the governors of your child's learning pace. Let them gobble down volumes of books. Let them explore physics as a 12-year-old. Let them dip their brains in the works of Shakespeare, Brontë, Aristotle, and Kant as soon as they'd like.

The way the system is structured can lead to children developing negative and toxic beliefs about themselves.

You hold the profound power of nurturing a beautiful mind with a steady, gentle hand through homeschooling. Part of seeing what's possible with this adventure called homeschooling is knowing you can speed up, slow down, or stop the train of learning at any time.

"But if I slow down or stop, how will my child do well on SATs or ACTs?"

We cover this in more depth later, but briefly, the SAT/ACT tests are not knowledge-based tests. They are logic and reasoning-based tests. And homeschoolers excel over their traditionally schooled peers in those areas.

Igniting a Fire versus Filling a Bucket

Do you ever look at your child and think, "My goodness, you are special." If you haven't done that lately, they're probably right next to you. Go on. Take a quick peek. Your child is remarkable, right? Not in a cheesy, Hallmark-card kind of way, although that is true, but rather, in an awe-inspiring wondrous way. You can just see their little minds churning and working right before they ask a question. More on that in a second . . .

The biggest difference I see with homeschoolers is that the goal of education is not the mere filling of a bucket, but the igniting of a fire, as first mentioned by the ancients.[1] The traditional school system expects our kids to be brim-full with all this information—facts, dates, numbers, and so on—and then, it's test time, so pour out everything you learned on the screen or test sheet. Didn't have enough in your bucket? That's a poor grade.

What happens if you try to overfill a bucket though? It sloshes and spills all over the place, wasting precious water that could have been used elsewhere. Some buckets that get overfilled too many times crack, break, and lose what makes them a bucket.

But we're just talking about buckets, right? Surely, we'd never see a bucket get overfilled so many times it simply cracks from pressure and expectations. Noooo . . . that would never happen . . .

What if, instead, we see our children's education like a fire to be fueled, not a bucket to be filled? If you want your child to thrive, why not give them the best fuel to go far, see amazing places, and cross paths with extraordinary people and opportunities?

There's some good value in the bucket-versus-fire comparison, but I contend that the problem goes much deeper than that. The school system bucket is being filled too high with comparative junk food. It's about malnourishment as much as it is about buckets.

Millions of children in the United States suffer from malnourishment. In many cases, it's not the absence of food, but instead, the presence of nutrient-deprived food. As much as I enjoy being a "foodie," that doesn't make me a nutritionist. As a mom though, I know what junk food does to my four kids' energy levels, focus, and overall health. Isn't it just as obvious what systematic deficiencies are doing to a multitude of children trapped in our schools? They're suffering from educational malnourishment, gross negligence for the performance we as a society demand from them on tests and grades.

The famous Victorian educator Charlotte Mason talked about the divine opportunity to feed a child's mind.

What if we see our children's education not like a bucket to be filled, but as a fire to be fueled?

"We don't want our children to have a feeble, starved intelligence. We want to nourish their minds . . . Thought breeds thought; children familiar with great thoughts take as naturally to thinking for themselves as the well-nourished body takes to growing; and we must bear in mind that growth, physical, intellectual, moral, spiritual, is the sole end of education."[2]

You give your child good food because you want them to be nourished. You give them fresh air, sunshine, vitamins, medicine, a good night's sleep, and plenty of exercise, because you know how much their body desperately needs that nourishment. The same necessity exists for your child's mind. As the stomach was designed to digest food, our minds are wired with a need to learn and grow, not simply to ingest and regurgitate. This is not just a preference, it is a deep need wired into our psychology from birth, first identified by Maslow in the 1940s,[3] then re-verified in 2011 by Diener and Tay.[4] Have you noticed that you don't have to encourage a child to learn to walk? And then, why you need to put child locks on your cupboards when they do?

You have the incredible gift and opportunity, with homeschooling, of cultivating your child's mind. How will you feed their mind for digestion? The secret is igniting in your child's heart an endless hunger for learning.

Fostering Inquisitiveness

Kids ask the *best* questions. I know, not the "But why, Mom?" question.

We've both had those days where we couldn't take another "Why?" question—but our kids *are* stuffed with amazing questions.

Classrooms, especially preschool and kindergarten classrooms, are the best places to see raised hands. "Oooh, oh, oh!" And what does the child often hear next? "We'll talk about that later," or "We don't have time for that today," or "That's not what we're talking about right now," and that question is *never* revisited.

How do I know? Because I was that teacher more than a few times. I can't believe I'm telling you this, but I remember being so focused on getting through my lesson plan as a teacher, that I would often say "later" or "not now" to my students . . . I was a meticulous teacher who took the state and school standards seriously. I was under a ton of pressure to stay on track. And I did. Often, that meant there was no time for asking great questions. No time for learning anything except what was exactly in my lesson plan. I'm so embarrassed now about this.

"Ugh, grace with yourself, Christy."

When you're told "No" enough times, you eventually stop asking . . . and the dream of hearing a "Yes!" wilts in your mind. Year after year, day after day, so many children in different classes and schools are told "No" by teachers, administrators, and other educators. Before you think I'm just picking on traditional schools, I know we, as parents, can say the same type of words, "No, not right now because I gotta do . . ."

> *The secret is igniting in your child's heart an endless hunger for learning.*

I don't know about you, but I can feel guilty sometimes when I tell any of my kids they need to wait for an answer. Sometimes it's necessary, don't get me wrong, but when I put myself in the shoes of the millions of kids who are in the system, they are told that all day long and often also at home. I do try to be mindful of my kids' curiosities. What redeems those times is remembering that homeschooling is made to honor your child as a person with their curiosities and intellect.

My son asked a question that stopped me in my tracks one day. A question about morality. It was a lightning bolt moment as I realized he was asking a question many people I know have struggled with for years. A struggle so severe I personally know friends and family who walked away from their faith and any sense of morality altogether by not finding a satisfying answer to this question. My son, at the time, was only 10, but this question challenges people of all ages and levels of intellect. It was serious.

It would have been easier to dismiss it with a short answer. I'll confess to doing that more than a few times, but this moment will stick with me for the rest of my life, and hopefully, his too.

When he asked his "mic drop" question, though we had a trillion things to do that day and a lot of lessons to get through, we stopped everything we were doing, and I made sure I was fully present with him. We talked through his question. I shared from my experience what other people I know have wrestled with when it came to this question, and then, we walked into our library and found some good books to help him.

It struck me at that moment that my son was searching for a rich meal of deep thought. My entire teaching plan for homeschooling him that day stopped to make space for that question. Would that have happened in a traditional school setting?

Maria Montessori once said,

> "Our aim is not merely to make the child understand, and still less to force him to memorize, but so to touch his imagination as to enthuse him to his innermost core."[5]

You are the best person in the world to spark your child's sense of wonder and curiosity every single day.

Nowhere do I see this so vividly experienced than when teaching one of my kids how to read. We grab some books, snuggle up on the couch with hot cocoa or tea, and tuck under a cozy, fluffy blanket. By the flickering of firelight, we flip open that first page.

You can just see the letters melding into words. Sounding out each part, blending those sounds into words, and boom, that flip of a switch when it all comes together! There is a *Every child should learn to read with snuggles on the couch.* joy, a brilliance in learning when I see my child read their first word on their own. Seeing that connection and my child's eyes light up is one of the most amazing experiences!

It breaks my heart to think there are parents who miss the joy of being there to see their child read for the first time. Why is that? There are countless parents, especially moms and maybe even yourself, who feel unqualified to teach their child to even read. That is a false belief, and I am so sorry if anyone has made you feel incapable of teaching your child how to read, because you can absolutely experience that joy together.

I've often said, "Every child should learn to read with snuggles on the couch." It marks their first significant academic challenge, and what a precious gift it is when a child has a beloved companion by their side during this journey.

In those tender moments of "couch cuddles" and the triumphant "lightbulb" reading moments, we are reminded of the enchanting essence of the homeschooling adventure—cultivating inquisitiveness with affection and warmth. Learning to read, a child's inaugural school hurdle, takes on a profound dimension when enveloped in love, comfort, and unwavering support. It's a testament to the boundless potential of homeschooling, where curiosity thrives, challenges become exciting adventures, and every "why" and "how" is welcomed with open arms.

From the earliest stages of learning to read to the complexities of advanced subjects, even older students discover their enthusiasm and curiosity kindled in an environment overflowing with love, comfort, and encouragement. Here, the act of learning to read is more than a mere skill; it transforms into a vibrant and positive experience. A supportive mentor, celebrating their every achievement, cultivates a nurturing atmosphere that fuels inquisitiveness in learners, propelling them to explore the realm of learning with profound wonder and eager anticipation.

Aligning Your Values

Have I told you about Deanna? She's a gal I once knew. A homeschooler. One day we were talking with some other acquaintances, and I was struck by what she told me about homeschooling. She said, "My sole reason for homeschooling is because I don't have the time to undo what's already been done with my kids the seven hours they've been at school."

I wish you'd been in that conversation because you would have instantly known what Deanna meant. She wasn't talking about undoing the academic part of schooling. No, she was talking about how their family values were unraveling day by day because of what her sons were being influenced to believe at school, in their classes, and by their peers.

Now, I've never been one to force my values on anyone, but our family's values are *essential* to how we live and enjoy our lives. You have values in your family, too. Do you expect your child's school to reinforce those same values when they're in school? Would you say your child is more aligned or less aligned with your family's values *because* of their experience at school? Is your child a better person because of their time at school, or have you noticed a drop off in values?

What I've learned working with thousands of families is there is a *massive* difference between default and design. You are either educating your child by default or by design. Here's a fact of life: All children get raised, whether you are there for it or not. Yes, I said it, your child is getting raised by someone or something or a combination, whether that's by you, your babysitter, Netflix, video games, their peers, their grandma, or their teacher.

Here's a fact of life: All children get "raised," whether you are there for it or not.

It's perfectly valid to desire an alternative path for your child's education, one that aligns with your priorities and goals. Embracing the freedom to educate children based on family values through homeschooling is a precious opportunity to share what we cherish most. It allows parents to impart their deeply held beliefs, traditions, and principles in a personalized educational setting. And no, this doesn't mean indoctrination. Indoctrination is an intentional inculcating of a particular set of beliefs, ideas, or values using a dogmatic approach that suppresses—even punishes—critical thinking, questioning, and dialog. Healthy value transmission, by contrast, invites and welcomes these things. With critics adamant about restricting homeschool freedoms, it begs the question—which side of the argument is really doing the indoctrinating?

Graduating Thinkers

Critical thinking can be defined as the ability to analyze, evaluate, and synthesize information and ideas in a thoughtful, logical, and independent manner. It involves challenging assumptions, considering diverse perspectives, recognizing biases, and arriving at well-reasoned conclusions.

While the concept of critical thinking is commonly acknowledged and promoted in traditional schools, its practical implementation is often limited or superficial. The nature of compulsory schooling often discourages independent thought in favor of conformity—students feeling pressure to align answers with what they believe is expected rather than engaging in genuine critical analysis.

For most of my years in education, I thought I was teaching critical thinking. I wasn't. Not in its true sense.

While schools may believe they are teaching critical thinking, the prevalence of standardized curricula, grading systems, and teacher-centered instruction often promotes conformity rather than fostering true independent thought. Mere exercises in comparing and contrasting without encouraging students to question assumptions or analyze multiple perspectives do not effectively develop free thinking skills.

To truly cultivate critical thinking, students need the ability to challenge prevailing ideas without the risk of getting a bad grade for doing so.

To truly cultivate critical thinking, education needs to prioritize student-centered learning, open-ended inquiry, and opportunities for students to engage in deep analysis, independent thought, and the ability to challenge prevailing ideas. And without the risk of getting a bad grade for doing so.

John Taylor Gatto spoke to this abandonment of learning on the altar of convenience:

> "School trains children to obey reflexively; teach your own to think critically and independently. Well-schooled kids have a low threshold for boredom; help your own develop an inner life so that they'll never be bored. Urge them to take on the serious material, the grown-up material, in history, literature, philosophy, music, art, economics, philosophy, theology—all the stuff schoolteachers know well enough to avoid."[6]

Homeschooling turns to face the music of inconvenient questions and thoughts. It doesn't shy away from challenging the status quo. Homeschooling, when done well, empowers your child to graduate as a thinker, not simply a student of approved agendas, with the grades to prove it.

What better place for your child to engage with meaningful values and virtues first than in the loving context of home? Every part of your home is a microclimate of learning, a safe arena where your child can be free to ask daring questions, share ideas, and stress-test the foundation of how your family chooses to live. What we're creating is an atmosphere of education as Charlotte Mason would say: "[T]he child breathes the atmosphere emanating from his parents; that of the ideas which rule their own lives."[7]

It also means you don't have to choose. You *can* set your child up for success through a great education *and* give them a great homeschooling experience at the same time. They don't have to endure bullying, go through the motions, suffer with an awful teacher, or all the other "accepted" challenges of being in a traditional school just so they learn what everyone else is learning.

Where Do We Go Next?

We've discussed the flexibility of homeschooling, the power it holds in nurturing critical thinking within the comforts of home, and we've addressed several common misconceptions that often surround this educational choice. But we haven't defined yet precisely what homeschooling is.

So, before we discuss the ins, outs, and some of the myths and hangups regarding homeschooling, let's lay down some groundwork: what exactly is homeschooling?

Remember This

- All humans learn different subjects at different paces. Homeschooling accommodates these differences, where traditional schools cannot.

- Where homeschools can ignite the fires of a love of learning, traditional schools extinguish them with torrents of wasted time.

- It's entirely valid to seek an educational approach that aligns with your family values; and this choice doesn't equate to indoctrination.

CHAPTER SIX

Understanding Homeschooling: What It Is and Why People Do It

"What is most important and valuable about the home as a base for Children's growth into the world is not that it is a better school than the schools, but that it isn't a school at all."
—John Holt[1]

"This is Christy. She homeschools because she used to be a teacher."

I turned to greet the two women I was being introduced to, silently pondering the hostess's choice to include this additional detail in my introduction. It was a familiar scenario, being introduced as a homeschooler, but the "because she used to be a teacher" part was a new twist.

Here I was, in the midst of a social gathering, with someone else offering an unsolicited explanation, or perhaps, a sort of preemptive qualifier. I couldn't help but wonder what made her introduce me in this way. Maybe, in her graciousness, she aimed to proactively address any misconceptions the other woman might have had about homeschooling. It could have been an effort to ensure that our conversation began on the right note, free from any potential biases or doubts.

Months later, at another party a woman asked me, "How long do you plan on sheltering your kids?" (There's nothing quite like the magical combination of a few drinks on an empty stomach to loosen the lips and get a backstage pass to what people are truly thinking.)

While it's always wise to give the benefit of the doubt, it's undeniable that people in our society harbor preconceptions about homeschooling. Whether comments are made innocently or not, the truth is that homeschooling, in some circles, has a negative reputation. I wish I could tell you that my homeschooling rarely comes up in social situations, and that these two conversations were unusual, but they are not. In fact, these questions and misconceptions about homeschooling are all too common in the world today. From trolls on social media to genuinely curious commenters, I encounter these types of questions every single day. What does that tell us? There are so many misconceptions about homeschooling:

- Do your kids have enough friends?
- Are you all Jesus freaks or Christian weirdos who are religious extremists?
- Homeschool kids only have friends exactly like them—there's no diversity in their friendships.
- Homeschoolers are stuck at home and never get out into the "real world."
- Aren't your kids just adopting your worldview without question? Sounds like brainwashing to me . . .
- Your kids aren't super awkward, are they?

- You must be Super Mom to homeschool your kids. I could never do that . . .

- How is your kid ever going to get accepted into college without an official transcript?

Some questions can be quite intriguing, while others might carry a weight of uncertainty that can sometimes leave homeschoolers, whether you're already on this educational journey or considering it, with doubt. If you're currently grappling with confusion about how homeschooling fits into your aspirations, let's go back to the essentials and establish a strong foundation from the start.

What Is *Homeschooling?*

Homeschooling is "the education of school-aged children at home or at a variety of places other than a traditional school setting." *Homeschooling* is also known as *home education* or *elective home education*. Same idea, different names. The important part is that you're guiding your child's education outside the structure of the traditional school system.

So, who usually does the educating? Oftentimes, the educator is a parent, tutor, and/or online teacher, and yes, you can trust several teachers to help educate your child. (No, you don't have to carry this responsibility all by yourself. More on that later.) Homeschooling typically uses a less formal, more personalized approach to education that is not often found in schools.

Homeschooling doesn't require a parent to be an expert in any subject

Homeschooling can take on many different forms, ranging from highly structured scheduling that's based on traditional school pedagogy to more open, freeform styles, such as unschooling.

Common Characteristics of Homeschooling

What does homeschooling typically look like? That's a loaded question, and yet, I hear this question at least a few times every week, if not every day. Generally speaking, the families I know and mentor typically have these characteristics in their approach to homeschooling.

1. Education is parent-guided.

Homeschooling empowers parents and caregivers to take control of their child's education. It doesn't require any one parent to be an expert in every subject or a super genius across all topics. With parent-directed homeschooling, you can source curricula without taking on so much in-the-trenches responsibility. Unlike a public school or even a private school setting, you still have control over who is actually teaching your child.

We homeschool because we know what our kids are consuming. You choose the curriculum. You choose the classes. You are the one with the ultimate say over who gets to teach your child.

2. Education is customized to meet a child's and family's needs.

You also get to guide the pace of the curriculum to fit your child's exact needs. What's your child's personality? What's interesting and engaging for your whole family? The traditional school system is obsessed with age- or grade-specific curriculum that shrinks the learning experience into a short window of time.

Homeschooling often throws off those ill-conceived, industrialized notions in favor of a more holistic approach to learning. What does your child need the most? What will nurture a stronger bond within your family? That's part of the beauty of homeschooling: your whole family, yes, even you, grandma or grandpa, can be a part of learning together.

3. Education can take a broader meaning beyond academics.

In more classical education circles, you'll find a greater emphasis on growing the mind, not uploading an entire library. Homeschooling families are known for using different methods to feed whole-brain development, cultivate virtues and build soft skills. Examples are handicrafts and hobbies, Latin and Greek, interest-led learning, socio-emotional health, and other amazing disciplines.

Education is far too important to be scrunched inside the confines of "academics." Homeschooling pops the ceiling off the limits of education to grow free and explore beyond any one subject or school year. The secret is in developing a lifelong love of learning, which we'll cover more of in a short while.

Homeschooling is a more holistic approach to learning—what does your child need most?

4. Education is primarily home-based, wherever that may be.

Whether you're on the road, online, or on the couch with a great book immersed in the tales of Alexander the Great, homeschooling is wherever home may be right now. We've homeschooled on road trips, at Airbnbs, at Grandma's house, and even at 35,000 feet in the air!

5. Educational choices are up to the parent, but still must comply with homeschooling laws.

Homeschooling is legal in all 50 states, but the laws differ in each state. Some states are what we would call "low regulation states" with little reporting to government authorities required while other states may be "high regulation" and have specific yearly requirements, such as standardized testing.

Whatever approach you decide to take with homeschooling, I cannot emphasize this enough—you need to know your legal obligations. The good news is the requirements are often simple and straightforward. If you ever get confused, there are some good legal organizations that can advocate for your homeschooling rights. For more guidance, please download my free "How to Homeschool Guide" waiting for you at christy-faith.com.

Homeschooling removes the ceiling from education, to freely explore beyond any one subject or school year.

One of the most exciting changes I've seen is how different the faces of homeschooling look today compared to 20 or even 10 years ago.

Why Are More Families Choosing to Homeschool Their Children?

After engaging with thousands of homeschooling and homeschool-curious families, I carefully documented the various motivations behind their interest in home-schooling. Through this process, I identified five primary categories that encompass the majority of reasons why families opt for homeschooling. As you explore these categories, you might find your own motivations aligning with some of them.

I want to emphasize that the following five main reasons are presented in a random order, not indicative of any personal preference or validation on my part. Each reason holds equal merit and is listed as such to provide you with a comprehensive understanding.

1. You want to further develop or preserve your family values.

Many homeschooling families choose to separate from the traditional school system based on their values. This decision often arises from a combination of concerns about the sociopolitical aspects embedded in the traditional school system and a desire to nurture different sets of values, principles, or priorities that may diverge from the mainstream blueprint.

It's important to note that this isn't exclusive to religious families; there are many secular homeschooling families that also share strong objections to certain aspects of what schools teach. For some homeschooling families, the motivation is to incorporate their socially conscious values, convictions, or cultural traditions into their child's education. Homeschooling offers the freedom to prioritize and emphasize subjects like cultural heritage, allowing families to instill these more deeply into their everyday educational experiences.

2. You want to improve and protect your child's health and safety.

Children are now graduating with PTSD because of trauma experienced at school.

"Christy, I can't even focus on my work knowing I could get that call at any moment of the day." I can't tell you how many times I've heard those types of words from parents around the world, but especially here in the United States. With the rise in gun violence on school campuses, more parents see homeschooling as a way to protect their child's well-being.

Layered on the visible risk of physical harm is a constant threat of social, emotional, and mental health dangers. Bullying, peer pressure, anxiety, depression, self-harm, and a score of other real risks are all rising in the traditional school system. Children are now graduating with PTSD because of these dangers at school.[2]

Are homeschooled students vulnerable to all these same mental and emotional risks? Of course, we would be foolish at best to assume the darker sides of technology and society somehow stop at our doorstep. However, as a parent or caregiver, you can be more in touch with what exactly your child is encountering throughout the day.

3. You want to have greater flexibility for scheduling, travel, and extraordinary opportunities.

Some of my earliest experience working with homeschooled children was through our learning center. Who were those students? A fast-rising ice skater, a Junior League surfer, and child actors whose faces and names I guarantee you've seen from favorite movies on every network or streaming platform.

Why were they homeschooled? To give their families greater flexibility to pursue a world-class skill or interest. If a child needed to be across Los Angeles for a 10:45 audition or table read, it was next to impossible to maintain a "normal" school schedule. The solution?

Homeschooling.

Maybe you have a unique lifestyle traveling to different countries every month while you run your drop-shipping company or lead your remote team. Maybe you're homesteading and want to know your kids are getting a great education while you build the life of your dreams. Maybe you're touring the open road with a newly furnished Schoolie (cute bus, by the way!) and want your child to have an unbelievable life experience instead of being chained to a desk for seven-plus hours.

Life is too short not to see how far you can go with homeschooling.

4. You want to foster a lifelong love of learning.

Is the traditional school system teaching your child how to learn or simply what to learn? It may surprise you that one out of every three U.S. high school graduates never reads another book after graduating.[3] The reason? I believe it's because their love for learning slowly wasted away while giving teachers exactly what they want. Why bother reading another book if it's not going to get you a better grade? If some extrinsic reward isn't attached, then what's the point?

One out of every three U.S. high school graduates never reads another book after graduating.

Families that choose to homeschool see learning as a divine gift. We get to learn and discover new ideas and exciting nuggets of knowledge buried in the dust of history. We get to take a page-gilded time machine to the far reaches of the universe and stretch our understanding. From da Vinci to Edison, Angelou to Aristotle, and Michelangelo to Sun Tzu, the sages of past civilizations can guide our learning if we would just let their wisdom transfer into our lives.

A lifelong love of learning is priceless as it fosters greater creativity, a more well-rounded perspective, and the chance to pursue what's interesting and worthy of mastery. By following passions and curiosities, learning becomes an exhilarating adventure rather than a compulsory obligation.

5. You want to give individualized instruction to your child.

Homeschooling provides a unique opportunity for individualized education, catering to the specific needs and circumstances of each child. For parents of children with special needs, homeschooling allows for tailored instruction and accommodations that can address their unique learning profiles. It provides a supportive environment where parents can closely monitor their child's progress, implement personalized strategies, and access specialized resources to help them thrive academically and emotionally.

Similarly, for parents of gifted children, homeschooling offers the flexibility to provide challenging and advanced materials, allowing these students to learn at their own accelerated pace and delve deeper into their areas of interest. Homeschooling also benefits students who may have faced difficulties in traditional school settings, such as those who require a flexible schedule due to medical conditions or those who have experienced bullying or social challenges. In all these scenarios, homeschooling empowers parents to create an individualized educational experience that nurtures their child's unique strengths, addresses their specific needs, and fosters a love for learning in a supportive and personalized environment.

I get visibly upset whenever I see or hear a traditional school educator, administrator, or doctor tell parents they are incapable of homeschooling a child because the child has ADHD, autism, or a different set of special needs. They say things like, "How could you possibly know how to educate your child? You're not trained in their diagnosis!" We'll cover more of this in Part 4 of this book.

For all homeschooling families, leaning into individualized instruction can open up a world of greater connection and confidence for your child. Homeschooling a more artistic-inclined child means you have the freedom to customize your classes to align with their artistic interests. History class can be a journey through ancient civilizations as you give greater context for the art skills they're developing. Writing can be a deep dive into the greatest sculptors throughout history.

The sages of past civilizations can guide our learning if we would just let their wisdom transfer into our lives.

Whatever you can imagine, there are ways to draw in your child's interests to co-shape their learning. You're giving your child the chance to develop skills or pursue subjects not typically taught in a traditional school setting.

A Variety of Diverse Pedagogies and Learning Methods Are Available

Homeschooling provides a unique opportunity to adapt and tailor the educational experience to the specific needs and interests of each child. It's about fostering a love for learning, nurturing curiosity, and instilling values that extend far beyond the confines of traditional education.

In this journey, flexibility is key, allowing you to explore various styles, combine elements, and ultimately, find what resonates best with you, your family, and your child. There is a great diversity available in teaching philosophies, structure and curriculum, including traditional schooling, Montessori, Waldorf, Classical, Charlotte Mason, Unit Studies, Unschooling, and Interest-Led styles. Or create your own custom "Eclectic" style by selecting learning experiences and curriculum from multiple styles.

In addition, there are many fun, productive ways you can partner with other families to create an Alternative Learning Community (ALC), such as participating in a micro school, cottage school, co-op, pod, or taking advantage of the Enrichment Programs and Online Homeschool Academies that are available.

The success of homeschooling lies not in the pursuit of a singular "perfect" style, but in the act of homeschooling itself.

Furthermore, live online classes offer a dynamic educational experience that extends beyond academics.

They provide a platform for children to socialize with peers from diverse backgrounds, cultures, and locations worldwide. Through these virtual connections, kids forge friendships, share ideas, and engage in collaborative projects, adding a vibrant and enriching dimension to their social lives.

Which of the homeschooling and/or styles and methods best prepare kids for the "real world"? The true success of homeschooling lies not in the pursuit of a singular "best" style, but in the act of homeschooling itself. It's the dedication, the personalization, and the genuine care invested in a child's education that truly make it work. From the highly structured traditional style to the more freeform unschooling style, all these methods can prepare children for the complexities of adult life.

In our rapidly evolving society, adaptability, critical thinking, and self-directed learning are paramount qualities. Homeschooling, in its diverse forms, instills these skills organically. By tailoring education to individual needs, children learn not just facts, but also how to approach challenges, solve problems, and pursue their passions. They become self-motivated learners, equipped with the ability to navigate a diverse and ever-changing world.

By its very nature, regardless of the style you choose, homeschooling education can easily extend beyond textbooks, fostering emotional intelligence, empathy, and a strong sense of self. It's a foundation that empowers them not just academically, but as

> *By tailoring education to individual needs, children become self-motivated learners, equipped with the ability to navigate a diverse and ever-changing world.*

well-rounded, capable individuals poised for success in any endeavor they choose to pursue. Our world needs all sorts of people with all sorts of skills, and homeschooling plays a crucial role in nurturing this diversity.

What's important for you to know is that you hold control. You can choose *whatever* style you want that fits what you, your family, and your child need the most. If you try a style and it isn't a fit, simply choose another style or mix and match and have fun exploring what works for you!

To help you identify homeschooling styles that are a best fit your family, I've developed a free 5-Minute Homeschool Style Finder. Simply head over to my website at Christy-Faith.com and look for the free resources.

When Your Child Turns Five, Do You Suddenly become Incompetent?

Homeschooling, a journey that offers the freedom to tailor your child's education to their unique needs, comes with moments of uncertainty. We've all been there, questioning our abilities as educators and parents. Think back to when your child was little. Who taught them how to tie their shoes? How to roll over, sit up, crawl, stand up, and walk? Who showed them how to use a cup, grab a spoon, or to pick up Cheerios with those chubby little baby hands?

Before your child was five years old, you taught them essentially everything they needed. Did you take off your parent hat and put on a teacher hat? No, of course not! You simply taught them, in the moment. And with so much love and patience that they knew you cared.

Parents are teachers. Period.

From the moment our kids are born, parents are teaching. We simply switch the topic or subject as our kids get older. The tragedy is there are many parents who are told they are no longer qualified to teach their kids as soon as their child turns five years old (when they reach school age).

I'll confide in you that there are plenty of days I'm still adjusting and refining homeschooling for our family. Do my 20 years as a professional educator help? Not as much as you might imagine. Home education is quite a different animal than traditional schooling. In addition to furnishing my kids with an academic education that prepares them for their future careers, I'm also nurturing their development with the goal that they become individuals who continue to learn, growing into capable, knowledgeable, and self-assured adults in the years ahead.

Remember This

- Most criticisms about homeschooling stem from misunderstanding what homeschooling truly is and why parents choose it.

- There are a variety of homeschooling styles and methods parents can use to curate the homeschool that is the perfect fit for their family and children.

- To find out more about the homeschooling styles, and which one best fits you, visit Christy-Faith.com and take my free 5-Minute Homeschool Style Finder.

PART FOUR

Insight into Homeschooling: Separating Fact from Fiction

Flipping the Script on Socialization: The Most Common Objection Is Our Greatest Strength

> Them: "Wow, your kids are so well mannered and friendly! Where do they go to school?"
>
> Me: "Why, thank you. We homeschool."
>
> Them: (anxious gasp of disapproval) "But what about socialization?!"

Let's talk about the boogeyman.

The trump card of anti-homeschoolers. Socialization.

It is the most common objection or concern people have about homeschooling. It may sound much like a well-meaning mother-in-law, sister, best friend, parent, or even that tiny little voice at the back of your mind . . .

> *"I want to homeschool, but I'm just so worried about my kid being socialized."*

Storytime.

So, there I was, with globs of brown dye being brushed into my hair, when the all-too-familiar question about socialization made its appearance once again.

This time, it came from the stylist next to me who had caught wind of my conversation with Chelsea, my trusted hairstylist of many years, about homeschooling. Seizing a momentary break between her own appointments, the neighboring stylist leaned in and politely inquired, "May I ask you something? I'd really love to homeschool my daughter but I'm just so worried about socialization."

A momentary pause hung in the air, her wide eyes fixated on me, brimming with genuine concern. As I glanced up at her, witnessing the unmistakable love she had for her daughter, something within me stirred, breaking the somewhat automatic pattern of me simply reciting my rehearsed defense of homeschoolers and homeschool socialization. I thought to myself, I have answered this question hundreds, if not thousands, of times, and despite what I tell this woman, right now, I can pretty much guarantee my answer will not strike a chord or alter her belief.

Perhaps it was the cocktail of chemicals resting on my scalp or maybe the salon fumes giving me a moment of clarity. In that second though, something switched, and I didn't mentally slide into a defensive stance. Instead, a thought popped into my head. I relaxed, leaned in, and asked her, "What does *socialization* mean to you?"

Her reply was what you would expect. "I want my daughter to have friends and to do sports and be a part of groups."

Now, of course, we know homeschoolers do all these things, too, and she's from Colorado, where homeschool groups and activities are as common as palm trees in Los Angeles. While she may not be aware of every social outlet available to her daughter, she certainly knows she has options. It was in that instant, when she made a list that *literally describes* the vibrant social lives of homeschoolers across the nation, I realized something.

I wasn't just facing one person's inquiry when it comes to homeschool socialization. It goes much deeper than that.

Society has a way of imprinting certain ideas into our minds, almost like they're etched in stone. These influences are incredibly powerful, shaping our thoughts, values, and perceptions from a young age. They create a sort of mental shield around our beliefs, making it tough for new information to break through. It's like we're caught in a web of societal conditioning, holding on to our convictions even when faced with evidence that suggests otherwise. So, when someone questions homeschool socialization, it's not just a simple conversation; it's a clash against strong forces that shape our collective mindset.

I would be remiss to write a chapter on homeschool socialization that only defended it with the same replies all of us have been using for years. Been there, done that. If we genuinely desire to transform societal perceptions of homeschool socialization, we must delve deeper into the underlying factors specific to homeschooling that contribute to these perceptions. The obvious arguments don't shift the narrative. We need to recognize that the go-to explanations and defenses, though valid, fall short in challenging the deeply ingrained prevailing misconceptions about homeschool socialization.

Shedding light on the phenomena of groupthink, risk-aversion, and confirmation bias are our first steps to gain insight as to why the facts aren't as persuasive as one might think they should be.

Groupthink: The Power of Slogans, Stereotypes, and Word Association

Throughout my years of studying history, both as an undergraduate and graduate student, one aspect that always captivated me is the incredible power of ideas. It's amazing how a single idea, when nurtured and spread, can shape the course of nations, influence societies, and profoundly impact the lives of individuals. Ideas have the remarkable ability to ignite revolutions, challenge established norms, and drive significant social and cultural transformations.

Slogans and stereotypes have played a powerful role in shaping collective thinking. When it comes to homeschool socialization, catchy slogans like "Homeschoolers are socially awkward" or stereotypes portraying homeschoolers as isolated and lacking in social skills are deeply ingrained in our society. These oversimplified narratives, although far from the truth, often go unchallenged due to the influence of groupthink.

For example, the stereotype of the "religious homeschooler" emerged from a confluence of historical and cultural factors. In the 1980s and 1990s, homeschooling gained increased attention and faced legal and social challenges. It was during this time that religious motivations for homeschooling gained prominence, with many conservative Christian families embracing homeschooling as a way to integrate their faith into their children's education. The media's focus on these religious homeschoolers contributed to the association between homeschooling and religious fundamentalism.

Despite the homeschool landscape being much more diverse, as we have shown earlier, this perception remains. There is a wide range of motivations for choosing homeschooling from tailoring academics to individualized learning, and addressing specific educational and socialization needs. And it may surprise some, but many families homeschool *because* of socialization. They view the school system as a place where self-esteem and confidence are whittled away.

Additionally, they want to shield their children from potential traumas like bullying, school shootings, and other distressing experiences, recognizing that these events don't actually "toughen kids up"' but can leave lasting negative effects.

When surrounded by societal pressures, it's easy to conform to prevailing beliefs about homeschool socialization, even in the face of contradictory evidence.

Groupthink, fueled by slogans and stereotypes, can create a powerful psychological force that reinforces misconceptions. When people are surrounded by like-minded individuals or subjected to societal pressures, it's easy to conform to prevailing beliefs about homeschool socialization, even in the face of contradictory evidence.

Associations, those clever connections between words, have an intriguing way of shaping our perceptions too. Think about it: when you hear *peanut butter*, your mind instinctively jumps to *jelly*, and *Wheaties* brings forth the image of the "Breakfast of Champions." But you know what? Just like how we don't immediately say "Bring in their Amazon packages while they're on vacation" when we hear "Like a Good Neighbor," there are certain words and slogans that permeate society. We need to acknowledge this.

The same goes for homeschooling and socialization. These associations greatly influence how we think, but here's the exciting part: we can untangle their influence! By digging deep and questioning these connections, we can gain a fair and accurate understanding of this "homeschool socialization" watch phrase.

Risk Aversion: The Dominance of Fear in Decision-Making

Humans are naturally wired to be risk-averse, as fear often drives decision-making processes. When it comes to challenging societal perceptions about homeschool socialization, the fear of deviating from the norm or being ostracized can be a powerful deterrent. Even when presented with compelling facts and figures demonstrating homeschoolers' positive social outcomes, individuals may hesitate to change their minds due to the fear of being perceived as unconventional or going against the grain.

Psychological studies have shown that the fear of losing is more motivational than the potential for gain. This phenomenon, known as loss aversion, can make individuals reluctant to reconsider their beliefs about homeschool socialization, as they perceive the potential loss of social acceptance or credibility outweighing the manifold benefits of embracing homeschooling.

The reluctance to consider homeschooling often stems from a well-intentioned, yet deeply ingrained, risk aversion.

This resistance, driven by cognitive and emotional factors, can make it challenging to accept new evidence supporting the effectiveness of home-schooling, even if it is well researched and statistically compelling. This is because it contradicts pre-existing beliefs about the risks associated with non-traditional education.

The crucial questions to ask are: (1) whether we possess the courage to reevaluate where the most significant risks lie concerning our children's education, and (2) whether we maintain an honest assessment about ourselves to see if we are holding on to any irrational fears. Recognizing the powerful role of risk aversion and its substantial influence on decision-making processes is essential when families are considering (and scared of) homeschooling.

> *The crucial questions to ask are: (1) whether we possess the courage to reevaluate where the most significant risks lie concerning our children's education, and (2) whether we made an honest assessment about ourselves to see if we are holding on to any irrational fears.*

Confirmation Bias: Clinging to Beliefs Despite Evidence

Confirmation bias can be a sneaky trap. We all fall prey to it from time to time. Regarding homeschool socialization, it's not uncommon to hear someone say, "Oh, I once knew a homeschooler, and he was socially awkward." And just like that, we latch on to that single example and let it solidify our belief that all homeschoolers must be socially inept. I chuckle when I hear this (and I hear it a lot) because

I started out teaching junior high. If anyone walks into a crowded junior high lunchroom, chances are they'll spot a socially awkward kid or two, without having to look very hard.

It's absurd to base our perceptions on a single anecdotal experience. Yet, that's exactly what confirmation bias does. It tricks us into clinging to information that confirms our existing beliefs while conveniently ignoring everything else, including empirical evidence. It's like putting blinders on and only seeing what we want to see.

Homeschooling, just like any other form of education, is a diverse landscape. There are homeschooled kids who are incredibly outgoing, confident, and socially adept. And yes, there are also introverts who clam up in a crowded room. That's true for students in traditional schools too! We need to recognize our human tendency toward confirmation bias, try our best to take those blinders off, and see this issue with a more open mind. Doing so, we will be more receptive to the data that shows homeschoolers statistically are thriving socially even more so than their traditionally schooled peers. Social health may look different than what you are used to seeing though, which brings us to the next, can't-ignore section.

The Uncomfortable Truth We Must Embrace

I'm just gonna come right out and say it. Some homeschoolers *are* different.

Everyone knows it. Everyone sees it. But not everyone knows what to do with it. The answer is not to quickly slap the "socially awkward" label on a child or teen just because they don't fit the cookie-cutter mold. It's like expecting a square peg to fit perfectly into a round hole. Homeschooled kids have their own unique social and academic culture that sets them apart, and that's something to be celebrated, not criticized.

Yet, despite our professed ideals of embracing uniqueness and individuality, we can't help but feel a sense of unease when we encounter kids who march to the beat of their own drum or like to talk about Tolstoy more than TikToks. It challenges our norms and triggers feelings of uncertainty. We start to worry and, let's be honest, we might even become a little judgy.

Perhaps, to truly understand and appreciate homeschooling, we need to reflect on our own experiences growing up in traditional schools. We must consider how our own insecurities and biases about being "different" influence our perception of homeschoolers, unfairly projecting our own fears onto a separate culture even though those concerns may not be relevant in that context.

Some homeschoolers are different. Everyone knows it. Everyone sees it. But not everyone knows what to do with it.

First, let's start by going back those years or decades to consider our own school experiences of how "different" kids are treated in schools. Most of us come from the traditional school system where "standing out" was a recipe for bullying, loneliness, and trauma. You didn't want to be that kid or have anything to do with kids like that.

This reminds me of Laura, who had the courage to share her story with me.

She had a classmate named Ethan who was on the "bigger side," poor, and not well cared for at home. He would often come into school with messy hair and smelling of cigarettes and unclean clothes.

Our insecurities and biases about being "different" influence our perception of homeschoolers, unfairly projecting our own fears even though those concerns may not be relevant in that context.

Laura got paired with him one day by their teacher and had a great time working with him in class. She confessed, "I did not want to work with him" as she already adopted the mindset of "you stay away from this kid." However, despite her initial disappointment she ended up having a fun time with him and decided to sit with him on the bus that day after school.

The next day, she recounted "I got all the teases!" Laura's classmates taunted her, "Ew, you have Ethan germs! Don't touch me! You like him! You love him! Ew, you're gross!" She relayed that her classmates even had a game where if Ethan touched you or something you owned, it now had "Ethan germs" and you had to go touch someone else as quickly as possible to get rid of them.

Laura shared,

> "I learned the lesson that day that you do NOT associate with Ethan and you fall in line, or else you, too, would become a victim. So, I never played with him again and I partook in all the nasty games and name-calling."

She admitted that from that day forward her classmates, including her, made his life miserable.

> "It was relentless taunting on a daily basis, and no one had his back."

Fast-forward to the present, and we are confronted with homeschooling. It seems good, really good. But bells start going off when a critic starts up with the anti-homeschool slogans like "Your kid is going to turn out weird if you homeschool."

The mere thought of having a "different" kid strikes fear deep within us.

The stereotypes and slogans tap into the painful memories of our own experiences or witnessing the struggles of those who didn't fit the mold during our school years. Suddenly, a seed of doubt is planted: What if my child doesn't turn out okay? This thought goes against every parent's heartfelt desire for their children. It's a self-perpetuating cycle of fear that keeps so many bound to the system, to the detriment of their own families.

I think for a lot of people the term *not being socialized* is code for what they are really dreading: "What if my kid doesn't fit in?" This could be yet another reason why, despite the fact that we can talk about our homeschooled kids' robust extracurricular and social lives until we are blue in the face, we still get nowhere.

> *The term* not being socialized *is code for what they are really dreading: "What if my kid doesn't fit in?"*

The ramifications of kids not fitting in or being socially awkward in our schools are terrifying, and people who are unfamiliar with homeschool culture, maybe even yourself, have no choice but to take that perspective. That's the only context we know! Probably we grew up in the schools ourselves and we've never been told otherwise (psst . . . that's why we're here).

What I love about homeschooling is that socialization is one of the big, hairy, scary fears *before* starting. Often once parents start homeschooling, this fear of not being

The good news is being "different" may be a taboo status to kids in the traditional school system, but it's often liberating and empowering for home-schooled kids.

"socialized" often turns into "Why did I ever worry about that?"

The good news is being "different" may be a taboo status for kids in the traditional school system, but it's often liberating and empowering for homeschooled kids. Why? Two reasons: (1) fitting in versus belonging, and (2) peer orientation.

A quick note: I'm not saying every single homeschooled kid is different, awkward or—insert your own word—or should be. My argument is two-fold:"

1. Because of the rich homeschool social culture and academic environment, it is understandable for a homeschooled kid to stand out; and honestly, this should not be surprising.

2. If a homeschooled kid does stand out, does it matter? They probably don't care, and you shouldn't either. There are many homeschooled kids who you never even notice because they present like any other kid on the block. I will say, however, that homeschool culture is so dissimilar to school culture it makes perfect sense if our kids look and act a little different.

The key differentiator we need to recognize is what we mean by "fitting in."

"Fitting In" Is Not the Same as "Belonging"

Brené Brown, the famous researcher, author, and speaker, talks about fitting in as being the opposite of belonging. Fitting in is assessing the situation, the room, or your environment, and figuring out how you need to act, how you need to behave, what you need to say, and what you need to wear, so that you don't stand out. So you will be like the rest. Fitting in requires superficiality and insincerity.

In her book *Braving the Wilderness: The Quest for True Belonging and the Courage to Stand Alone*, Brown defines *belonging* in this way:

> "Belonging is the innate human desire to be part of something larger than us. Because this yearning is so primal, we often try to acquire it by fitting in and by seeking approval, which are not only hollow substitutes for belonging but often barriers to it. Because true belonging only happens when we present our authentic, imperfect selves to the world, our sense of belonging can never be greater than our level of self-acceptance."[1]

One could argue that the more effort a student makes to fit in, the more insecure they are. This means you can look, act, talk, and dress just like your peers and completely fit in, and still suffer from profound loneliness. No one knows any better because, for all intents and purposes, you are "socialized."

In our schools, children face a harsh reality: a high-stakes game with life-or-death odds. Conform, or face consequences. It's not just disheartening; for many young minds, it's the precursor to anxiety, depression, risky behavior, and tragically, worse. Homeschooled children are spared this pressure-cooker environment that demands conformity. Their self-assuredness may appear

You can look, act, talk, and dress just like your peers and completely fit in, and still suffer from profound loneliness. No one knows any better because, for all intents and purposes, you are "socialized."

"different" to those entrenched in this unhealthy need to blend in. What homeschoolers see as a healthy self-identity can sometimes be misinterpreted by others as "weird." How did our schools get to be this way? There are several reasons I can think of, but the most interesting one to me related to socialization is peer orientation.

The Dangers of Peer Orientation

Ever read a great book that gives you a lightbulb moment about a different topic? That happened to me when reading Gordon Neufeld and Gabor Maté's brilliant work *Hold on to Your Kids*. Neufeld and Maté argue that

> "For the first time in history young people are turning for instruction, modeling, and guidance not to mothers, fathers, teachers, and other responsible adults but to people whom nature never intended to place in a parenting role—their own peers."[2]

Peer orientation is so saturated in our culture today, we as parents hardly even notice. Those who do notice this often don't think it's an issue. I've talked about this publicly and I always get responses from well-meaning parents, psychologists, and other professionals,

> "Christy, attaching to peers and separating from parents is a normal developmental phase!"

To which I respond,

> "Just because something is normative does not mean it's healthy."

The argument goes like this: the most important people in children's lives should be the parents, because parents can best provide unconditional love, nurturing, guidance, and modeling; but they are being replaced by a much more unhealthy group: a child's own peers. The research is clear that, developmentally, children need a safe "compass point" for morality and sensible function as future adults. When one is not provided, they will find one for themselves.

Kids are wired for attachment. Unfortunately, children and teens today look more to their peers to meet their attachment needs, and it has proven to be a disaster because they are being conditioned to listen to the fragile immaturity of those who have neither the wisdom nor the experience to warrant this influence.

There is nothing healthy about peer orientation. Those who dare to seek out healthy attachment with their kids, so their kids can better navigate peer relationships, are often called "sheltering parents." Ensuring that your child is oriented to your leadership rather than to their peers' is not sheltering—it is gifting them with resilience.

The increase in peer orientation in our culture is linked to increased suicide rates among kids.[3] When studying teens who attempted suicide, the primary motive toward suicidal inclinations wasn't unhappy home lives, as many of us would think. When these kids were interviewed "the key trigger for the great majority was how they were being treated by their peers, not their parents."[4]

> *Children and teens today look more to their peers to meet their attachment needs, and it has proven to be a disaster.*

The bottom line is the more that peers matter, the more traumatizing it is when those peers reject you.

> "Fitting in with the immature expectations of the peer group is not how the youth grow to be independent, self-respecting adults . . . peer orientation undermines healthy development."[5]

When you don't fit in with the group that matters most to you, rejection and ostracization are your worst nightmares.

Ensuring that your child is oriented to your leadership rather than to their peers' is not sheltering—it is gifting them with resilience.

With the sheer amount of time kids are around other kids, it is extremely difficult to escape peer orientation. It's important to note here I'm not talking about kids having friends. Of course, we love friends. Having healthy friendships and having the disorder of peer orientation are two separate concepts.

Brené Brown's research on fitting in versus belonging and Neufeld and Mate's research on peer orientation present three undeniable truths:

1. We live in a society where peer orientation, as unhealthy as it is, is the norm.

2. We live in a society where we send our kids to a social environment saturated with their peers daily.

3. In a peer-oriented culture, fitting in is required to avoid bullying and ostracization.

Sadly, our society believes this structure is the necessary means for your child to be socialized. How. Very. Sad. Let's take a closer look at how homeschoolers truly "socialize" and see if we can realign that word to fit a healthier definition.

Exploring the Social Experience of Homeschoolers

Rebecca tried talking with her son's teacher. No change. She spoke with the administrator. Still no change. She finally got a meeting with her son's principal.

Her son was being bullied incessantly and she pled her case before the most influential person in the entire school. The principal's response? "That's unfortunate. If there's anything I can do about it, please let me know."

I wish I could tell you I was shocked when Rebecca shared this story. Unfortunately, her experience of not getting the help she needed from her son's school administration is the norm, not the exception, especially in the public school system.

We need to be realistic with recognizing that any time you mix a group of people (kids or adults) you will get some unpleasant "stuff." One of the great benefits of homeschooling is though these problems exist, it is on a much smaller scale and can be more easily addressed.

I remember a few years back we were in a co-op and some girls formed a clique. They were awful to another girl and though the mom tried to work things out, it never really got better. What did this mom do? The following year she found another community. In the homeschool culture parents and kids have more freedom to remove themselves from toxic environments.

Now, I know what you may be thinking, "Christy, how are you going to toughen them up?" to which I ask, "Toughen them up for what?"

Let's cut to the chase—the notion of "toughening up" is misplaced. The stark reality is, institutional peer-driven schools offer a unique and often harsh environment seldom replicated

The school environment may indeed prepare kids, but only to adapt and survive the unhealthy environment within its own walls.

Trauma and abuse don't cultivate resilience; rather, they inflict deep emotional wounds and stifle growth.

in adult life. The school environment may indeed prepare kids, but only to adapt and survive the unhealthy environment within its own walls. Advocates of homeschooling recognize that the notion of "throwing our kids to the wolves" to toughen them up for a so-called "real world" is flawed; this world, as it's commonly portrayed, doesn't truly exist. Instead, our focus should be on equipping kids with the ability to discern between healthy and unhealthy behavior. Trauma and abuse don't cultivate resilience; rather, they inflict deep emotional wounds and stifle growth.

Age Mixing

When children are segregated by age, our society robs them of an academically and emotionally robust education. Let me explain . . .

Academically, when you have a classroom full of 7-year-olds, there's only so much they know and understand. There is a limit to how far thoughts and intellectual capacities can go in that closed ecosystem. However, when you mix ages, those 7-year-olds can be exposed to more advanced concepts that, for example, a 10-year-old might introduce.

This holds true both in academic settings as well as within the context of play. Children experience a dynamic they would never have been exposed to or learn from if they were strictly segregated into associating with their own ages.

Kids also love having role models to admire. It is a beautiful gift when there is a respectable older person in a young kid's life with whom they can learn and with whom they can interact. This can happen in a co-op setting, or simply within your own family.

Birth order tendencies get stretched in a healthy way with age mixing too. In a family, the youngest is always the youngest and the oldest is always the oldest—and consistently treated as such. When you mix ages in a learning environment, that gives the oldest an opportunity to be younger and the younger one an opportunity to be older. Think of all the lessons you can glean from that switch of roles!

Practically speaking, here's how age mixing plays out. An older child, who is 10, has an opportunity to learn and play alongside a 5-year-old sibling and take a leadership role they would never experience otherwise. Likewise, for the younger child, age mixing allows them to learn from, emulate, and look up to an older child. This dynamic carries on when the family heads to the weekly co-op where the players and ages are mixed up and a new set of interactions come into play.

Age segregation is one of the travesties of our educational system that few talk about or even question, and it is far more influential than many even realize.

Age mixing gives all kids the opportunity to be the mentor and a mentee, to be a teacher and the student, and to be a role model and emotional support for a younger child. It nurtures a fresh appreciation for empathy and an understanding of others the child wouldn't otherwise cultivate in the confines of the grade-leveled school system.

Age segregation is one of the travesties of our educational system that few talk about or even question, and it is far more influential than many even realize. It is limiting our kids' education in ways I don't think we can even fathom.

Interactions with Adults

Homeschoolers flip the script on socialization in one remarkable way: through their engaging conversations with adults. While conventional wisdom may assume that social skills develop solely through interactions with peers, homeschoolers defy this notion. By engaging in meaningful dialogues with adults, homeschoolers showcase a level of conversational prowess that often surprises and impresses.

Drawing from their unique experiences and learning environment, they can effortlessly navigate discussions; demonstrating maturity, depth, and a genuine interest in connecting on a deeper level. Unlike the many schooled kids who view adults primarily as authority figures (not their fault, but undeniably true), homeschoolers often look to and embrace adults as valuable sources of knowledge, insight, and mentorship. This distinct approach to socializing fosters a rich and meaningful exchange that transcends the notions of what healthy socialization means.

To fluidly and appropriately socialize with a 1-year-old baby one minute and a great-grandmother the next is a beautiful hallmark of a well-socialized child.

To fluidly and appropriately socialize with a 1-year-old baby one minute and a great-grandmother the next is a beautiful hallmark of a well-socialized child. It's a different culture, and a difference I gladly embrace.

The Academic Experience of Homeschoolers

Academic experience also affects how homeschoolers relate to the world.

It's common for homeschoolers to:

- Read different books than their schooled friends

- Learn classical languages

- Have a lot of freedom in their day

- Make academic decisions with their parents

- Be accustomed to an environment with mixed ages, including adults

- Take different types of classes, such as logic and rhetoric and nature study

- Enjoy more interest-led learning

- Do a lot of learning outside of the home, not the once or twice a year field trip

Homeschooled kids are assessed differently as well (not always), but I don't know a single homeschooling mother who gives chapter and unit tests all the time. We are right there, sitting next to our kids, and engaging in meaningful conversations. We don't need tests every time to make sure our kids are well-educated.

In traditional schools, children do not have many of these experiences.

They are split up in classrooms according to age (and sadly, ability too). They are told what they need to learn with little to no input or discussion. They are forced to learn the material in one style (the "traditional style") regardless of whether it's best for them. They experience continual assessments and tests to prove they know what they are "supposed" to know. Worst of all, they're trained not to ask questions.

Characteristics of Healthy Socialization

So, if the schools aren't giving our kids healthy socialization, what exactly is it then? In my view, there are 13 essential characteristics to healthy socialization, and notably, none of these necessitate a traditional school environment for cultivation.

1. **Active Listening:** Paying close attention to others when they speak, showing genuine interest in their thoughts and feelings, and responding appropriately.

2. **Empathy:** Trying to understand and share the feelings of others. This helps in building connections and showing support.

3. **Communication Skills:** Clearly expressing oneself, both verbally and nonverbally, while respecting others' opinions and boundaries.

4. **Respect:** Treating others with consideration, kindness, and politeness, regardless of differences in opinions or backgrounds.

5. **Boundaries:** Understanding personal boundaries and respecting the boundaries of others. This helps maintain healthy and respectful relationships.

6. **Conflict Resolution:** Learning how to address conflicts in a constructive manner, focusing on finding solutions rather than blaming or escalating the situation.

7. **Shared Activities:** Engaging in activities or hobbies with others that you both enjoy, which can serve as a basis for forming connections.

8. **Seeking Common Ground:** Finding shared interests or values with others, which can help build rapport and establish a foundation for friendship.

9. **Joining Social Groups:** Participating in clubs, organizations, or community events can provide opportunities to meet like-minded individuals.

10. **Volunteering:** Working together towards a common cause can help in building camaraderie and fostering a sense of community.

11. **Online Interaction:** Engaging in online forums, social media, or interest-based communities are a way to connect with others who share similar interests.

12. **Self-Confidence:** Having a healthy sense of self-worth and self-assuredness can make social interactions more comfortable and enjoyable.

13. **Patience:** Building meaningful relationships takes time. It's important to be patient and not rush the process.

Quality Not Quantity

Throughout history, humans have thrived in close-knit communities and smaller social circles. These environments provided a sense of belonging, mutual support, and the opportunity for deeper, more meaningful connections. Consider, for example, villages or neighborhoods where people of various ages collaborated in their daily lives, sharing experiences and values.

In today's fast-paced world, however, socialization has become synonymous with the notion of extensive social exposure. Parents may feel compelled to fill their children's schedules with a multitude of activities and play dates, under the assumption that more equals better. Yet, the truth is that the quality, not the quantity, of social interactions holds greater significance.

For instance, a single meaningful conversation with a trusted friend or mentor can offer more profound insights and support than a series of fleeting interactions with a large group. Similarly, children can develop strong bonds and critical social skills through consistent, well-balanced interactions with a few close friends, rather than being constantly surrounded by a multitude of forced acquaintances.

Moreover, time spent alone or in quiet reflection should not be underestimated in the realm of healthy socialization. These moments of solitude foster self-awareness, creativity, and emotional intelligence—qualities that are essential for forming meaningful connections with others.

Many homeschooling parents, having experienced the traditional system themselves, grapple with the temptation to overload their children with activities. The conventional belief that children must spend most of their waking hours in large groups of peers with similar age and development levels is hard to shake.

The undeniable truth we must acknowledge is that a homeschooled child who exudes self-assuredness possesses a unique quality. I am immensely moved when I observe a homeschooled child or teenager interacting with the world, particularly with individuals of a different age (younger kids, adults, and seniors) with confidence, wisdom, and a keen intellect. This difference inspires hope that we can redefine and shape a future where we nurture a more whole understanding of socialization.

In today's fast-paced world, extensive social exposure has become synonymous with socialization. Parents feel compelled to fill their children's schedules with a multitude of activities and extracurriculars under the assumption that more equals better. Yet, the truth is that the quality, not the quantity, of social interactions holds greater significance.

Remember This

- If a homeschooler presents differently from traditionally schooled peers, it does not necessarily mean they aren't socialized. In fact, homeschoolers tend to be more intellectually, socially, and emotionally mature.

- A peer-oriented child is not a healthy child.

- Forced association, which is what schools provide, does not equate to socialization.

- A child who seems to effortlessly "fit in" and raises no social concerns may be the loneliest and most hurting individual in the entire school.

CHAPTER EIGHT

Hitting the Books: Educational Myths about Homeschooling

"The function of education is to teach one to think intensively and to think critically. Intelligence plus character - that is the goal of true education."

—Martin Luther King Jr.[1]

While it's clear that homeschooled students often excel beyond their traditionally schooled peers, I recognize that you might have legitimate concerns about academics in the homeschooling context. You might be wondering about maintaining consistent progress, effectively instructing across various subjects, and managing children of different grade levels. Let's explore these subjects and debunk some of the prevalent misconceptions surrounding homeschoolers and their academic accomplishments.

Myth: "Homeschoolers Are behind Academically"

The second-most common reason why U.S.-based families choose to homeschool is poor academic performance in the traditional school system.[2] We discussed some specifics earlier in the book, but just to summarize and refresh:

- On average, one out of every three students in fourth and eighth grades scored below NAEP's lowest level in math or reading, and the scores continue to decline.
- Homeschoolers consistently outperform their school system peers in literacy, standardized tests, SAT/ACT, college grades, and college graduation rates.

This raises a crucial question: if the primary objective of traditional schooling is academic progress, why does it frequently fall so short? It hints at underlying complexities within the conventional educational framework that merit examination.

Conversations with parents, much like the insightful discussion I had with my friend just yesterday, shed light on a significant observation. Some children grapple with thriving in the conventional classroom setting. This underscores the vital point that not all learning environments are universally effective.

Homeschooling presents a unique advantage—a tailored approach that addresses each child's distinct needs.

Moreover, it's not uncommon for children who were once deemed "falling behind" in traditional schooling to flourish within a homeschooling environment. This paradigm shift uncovers a crucial insight: when students fall behind, the challenge isn't always inherently with the failures of the child, but often with the structural limitations of the traditional school system.

Now, let's delve into a common concern: the fear of children lagging "behind" in their education. To truly address this apprehension, we must first consider what it means to be "behind." It's a question that warrants exploration—behind compared to whom? The apparent answer is in comparison to non-homeschooled students. Yet, the less evident answer lies in the standards set by the traditional education system. While I do not endorse standardized testing as

When a student falls behind, the challenge is often not the child but the school structure. A striking number of these children flourish when homeschooled.

the sole measure of a child's progress, it's worth noting that when evaluated in this manner, homeschoolers consistently excel. If we are to use standardized test performance as the measuring stick, it becomes evident that homeschooled students often surpass their traditionally schooled peers.

Evaluating the data, we find that 11 out of 14 national studies comparing homeschooled students to their public-schooled peers, based on standardized testing, demonstrate superior performance among homeschooled students. That's an impressive 78% success rate. And before any concerns arise, it's worth noting that for the remaining three studies, homeschooled students performed on par with their counterparts in traditional schools.

What's truly noteworthy is that homeschooled students don't merely score higher; they often achieve between 15% and 30% more points on standardized tests compared to public school students.

If you're apprehensive about your child's academic progress, rest assured, you're not alone. This is a legitimate concern, rooted in a deep desire to equip your child for a successful future. Remember, you don't have to navigate this journey in isolation. Dispelling myths about home-schoolers' academic achievements is only the beginning.

Let's keep moving on . . .

Myth: "Professionals Are the Only Ones Qualified to Teach, Especially Kids with Special Needs"

After spending the majority of my career supporting the traditional school system, I can tell you this belief is certifiably false. Our learning center team developed a small mountain of academic plans for thousands of students. I can tell you for a fact there is little that educators are trained to do that is difficult for a loving, motivated parent to master.

Homeschooling can be an ideal option for children with special needs because it allows for individualized attention, customized curriculum, and flexibility to accommodate their unique learning styles and pace. As a parent, you have the advantage of being intimately familiar with your child's needs, strengths, and challenges, which positions you as the best advocate and teacher for them.

Additionally, there is a wealth of specialized resources, support groups, and online communities specifically designed to assist homeschooling parents of children with special needs.

> *There is little that educators are trained to do that is difficult for a loving, motivated parent to master.*

While homeschooling provides many advantages for children with special needs, it's important to acknowledge there are certain specialized services the public school system offers through professionals. These services, such as speech therapy or occupational therapy, often require the expertise of trained professionals who can provide specific interventions and therapies tailored to a child's individual needs. While a parent can certainly implement most if not all accommodations and strategies outlined in an Individualized Education Program (IEP) at home, accessing these professional services may require seeking external support.

Fortunately, there are equivalent, and even superior, options available to supplement homeschooling, such as seeking services from private practitioners, enrolling in specialized therapy programs, receiving services from the local school district itself, or collaborating with community resources to ensure your child receives comprehensive support.

Homeschooling empowers parents to create a customized and nurturing setup, and with the right combination of resources, support, and dedication, you can provide your child with a well-rounded educational experience that addresses their unique needs.

Learning disabilities are not a reason to put your kid in school—it's often an even greater reason to opt out of the traditional school system.

Heather's son Micah was born prematurely at 27 weeks. It's difficult for any parent to imagine the unique challenges and emotions that come with such an experience. Even six years later, Micah had quite the team of medical advisors. A neuro-development pediatrician told Heather that a traditional school setting would be best for Micah because "You don't know enough to know if he's behind or where he should be academically. A real school setting will motivate

Micah more because he can see what the other kids are doing and how successful they are."

I've encountered objections from influential voices in the education space who question whether parents, particularly those with children who have special needs, can effectively teach at home. They challenge the notion of parents stepping into this domain and assume that it's beyond their capability. These doubts and concerns are not uncommon, but they don't define your potential as a dedicated parent, to not only meet the challenge, but raise the bar.

But let's consider this: Who is it who would dare to assert that you can handle this? It's the same loving parent who has likely been with that child for every doctor's appointment, specialist's follow-up visit, blood test, neurology exam, physical therapy and occupational therapy, and other twists and turns along the way. I see you. I can feel how much you care about your precious child. I hear it in your voice every day how much you love your child and how much you've fought for them to have a better future, a "good" life, whatever that means to you.

Others' doubts and concerns don't define your potential to meet this challenge; no one will fight for your child's progress like you will.

No one will fight for your child's progress, turning over every rock to find the best possible answers, and care for them like you will. And if you can't do it yourself, you will find the people to help, as Heather did.

A quick note about IEPs (Individualized Education Plans): when you read IEPs, they list accommodations that schools and educators are to implement for that child. Other than therapies, such as speech therapy and occupational therapy, most if not all classroom accommodations can easily be implemented at home. Here are 20 of the most common IEP accommodations I saw:

1. Extended time for assignments, tests, or exams

2. Preferential seating

3. Modified assignments or assessments

4. Assistive technology

5. Note-taking assistance

6. More frequent breaks or movement opportunities

7. Modified grading or evaluation criteria

8. Specialized instruction or support

9. Behavioral supports

10. Additional support from paraprofessionals or aides

11. Visual aids or graphic organizers

12. Use of manipulatives or hands-on materials

13. Individualized learning goals or objectives

14. Access to a quiet or low-distraction environment

15. Support for organizational skills and executive functioning

16. Use of sensory accommodations (fidget tools, noise-canceling headphones, etc.)

17. Extra help or tutoring sessions

18. Individualized behavior plans or behavior management strategies

19. Communication supports (visual schedules, communication boards, etc.)

20. Collaboration and communication with parents, teachers, and other professionals

Moreover, numerous IEP accommodations, such as extended test time, a calm workspace, and more frequent breaks, are specifically designed to address challenges within the classroom setting. When you transition your child out of a disruptive classroom environment, you may find that many of these accommodation needs simply disappear.

Many of the nontherapeutic accommodations are not complicated whatsoever and don't even apply when your child is removed from a traditional classroom setting. Remember that. The system focuses on getting kids on track with *their* standards, but what if your child doesn't fit that box? What if your child needs a different structure that fits their needs? The best opportunity may be to pair the homeschool learning experience with intervention specialists. The type of attention you can oversee and provide will never happen in a system that is primarily concerned with fixing your child's academic progress.

When you remove your child from a disruptive classroom environment, many accommodation needs often simply disappear.

You are the expert on your child. Bottom line.

Myth: "I Don't Have the Time to Teach a Full School Day"

Ask any teacher and they will tell you that large chunks of their day are lost to crowd control and administrative jockeying. It does not take seven hours to learn the material that actually gets covered in a school day. It can be done often in a couple of hours depending on your child's age and your homeschooling style *if* you're intentional with your time.

I can confidently affirm that homeschooled children can effectively cover their academic requirements in approximately half the time, or even less, compared to a traditional "full" school day. Even when engaging in online classes, any additional work assigned still comfortably fits within these hours. Those who pursue a more rigorous homeschooling curriculum, such as classical homeschooling, may approach the higher end of the time scale, yet they still typically fall considerably short of the traditional seven-hour school day. Figure 8.1 is my recommended chart for estimating the time your homeschooled child may need to devote to their studies.[3]

The best part? This includes homework, if your home-schooled child even has homework. When the schoolwork is done, it's done.

By establishing clear expectations, you can guide your child in structuring their day for effective and sustainable learning.

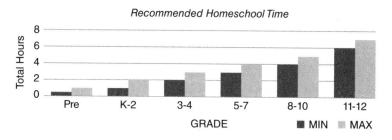

FIGURE 8.1 The time your homeschooled child may need to devote to their studies.

Homeschooled children can effectively cover their academics in roughly half the time of traditional school, or even less.

Some children thrive by tackling math facts as a priority in the morning, while others may benefit from a day-specific checklist. For instance, certain subjects might be scheduled for Tuesdays and Thursdays, while others are reserved for Mondays, Wednesdays, and Fridays. This tailored approach ensures that each child's learning style and pace are taken into account.

I need to let you in on one of the best-kept secrets in the homeschooling world. It's called outsourcing. Many folks just starting out homeschooling don't realize they don't have to teach every class or subject. Rest easy, we have the option to seek out and find world-class experts to teach things like AP Bio or Calculus. And yes, you're still in the driver's seat since you are determining who, how, and when it will be taught. There is a world full of learning resources, curricula, online academies, tutors, subject-matter experts, and crowdsourced libraries that are even academically superior to what's presented in the traditional school system today.

A key detail is giving your child the structure they need to learn with their preferred learning style that fits their personality. You have the power to try a few different approaches and find what fits you, your child, and your family's needs.

Myth: "It's Too Hard to Teach Multiple Kids in Different Grade Levels"

I talk with parents all the time who go from homeschooling one child to homeschooling multiple children all at once.

This is a source of significant anxiety for many homeschool parents. Why? Because we somehow have this idea in our minds that we're now the teachers standing in a classroom full of kids, all bubbling with energy and surrounded by distractions, and we have the unenviable task of coming up with all the answers and teaching *every* subject with stellar competence . . . or die trying.

This is simply not true for three reasons.

First, with as many subjects as possible, homeschooling families can thrive when multiple kids are all learning together. We call these "family together subjects." Many homeschoolers do family together subjects in the morning (we call this "Morning Time"), but it doesn't have to take place in the morning.

Morning time or a special block in your day for family together subjects can be an amazing bonding ritual as a family.

In fact, there are even homeschool curricula written specifically to incorporate multiple grade levels into the learning experience. As one example, with intentional planning, a kindergartener, a third grader, and a middle schooler can all learn about the Persian Empire at different levels in the same context. The kindergartener can do a coloring sheet with different objects that are specific to the historical context. The third grader can do an oral narration (summary) of the story. The middle schooler can do a writing assignment or put together a presentation about the topic. This is a basic explanation just to get the idea across, but you could even take this as a lesson plan if you want.

Second, when you do teach multiple ages together, as different-age children interact, they absorb concepts and ideas at a faster, more advanced level.[4] You don't have to do it this way, but the "one-room schoolhouse" approach is highly effective for many homeschool families. There is beauty in younger and older children interacting in a learning context. Older children get to model what they're learning with younger children, sharing their knowledge to help teach the topic.

Younger children can advance their learning beyond their limited comprehension which stretches their imagination, scope of learning, knowledge, and creativity. By the way, this interaction makes subjects like science, history, literature, and reading aloud incredible experiences for kids!

When you teach multiple ages together, they interact and absorb concepts and ideas at a faster, more advanced level.

Third, even if you don't want to group your kids for subjects, you can still set up your homeschool to run efficiently using well-known scheduling methods. For example, blocking out separate times for family-together subjects, independent study subjects, and "I do this with mom or dad" subjects.

Myth: "We Need to Trust Educational Experts to Decide What Kids Learn"

We live in a society where we're told to trust the experts for everything. But when it comes to our children's education, how wise is it to hand over the reins completely? Who knows your child better than you do? Who sees their strengths, passions, and areas of growth every single day? You do.

As a parent, you have the unique ability to tailor your child's education to fit their individual needs. Trusting educational experts can be important, but it doesn't mean we should ignore our intuition and blindly rely on them to decide what our kids should learn and when. We can combine their expertise with our deep knowledge of our children to create a truly powerful educational experience.

Imagine your child has a burning curiosity about astronomy. They spend hours studying constellations, devouring books about the universe, and dreaming of exploring space someday. But the standard curriculum barely scratches the surface of astronomy. So, are we supposed to stifle their passion and tell them, "Sorry, but the experts don't think that's important"? Absolutely not!

Homeschooling allows us to nurture their interests, dive deeper into subjects our kids are passionate about, and provide them with opportunities for real-world learning. If spending time studying astronomy pushes learning about semicolons back a few months, it doesn't mean your child is behind. It means you made a different choice (and probably the best one).

Now, I'm not saying we should disregard the expertise of educational professionals. However, it's important to remember they don't have a monopoly on knowledge. There are countless resources available to us as homeschooling parents, many of which are amazing and don't follow state standards; including many designed by other educational professionals with a paradigm that may be closer to yours. Does that mean your child isn't getting a great education? Of course not, especially if you are a homeschooler who does not follow the traditional style. You can sequentially use a curriculum, year by year, and your child will receive an incredible education, even if it doesn't follow standards.

If studying astronomy pushes learning semicolons back a few months, it doesn't mean your child is behind. It means you made a different choice (and probably the best one).

Trusting ourselves as parents doesn't mean we reject expertise; it means we are choosing a different path. And we're playing the "long game" too. So rather than compare your child to other kids by their year and month (like I used to do when I tested kids) let's step back and rest in the fact that over the long haul, they will learn all they need to know in the right time.

Myth: "Your Child Will Not Be Prepared to Take the SAT or ACT If They're Homeschooled"

Despite the myth the SAT and the ACT are on their way out, approximately 80% of four-year colleges and universities require ACT and/or SAT scores for admission.

I could tell you story after story of students academically at the top of their class, who bombed their first SAT or ACT exam. That's when they showed up at our learning center.

Moment of truth: how well do homeschoolers actually do on the "big two" tests? Homeschooled students typically score above average on the SAT and ACT tests that colleges consider for admissions.

"What?! Christy, no, that can't be true . . ."

The ACT reports that homeschooled students typically score an average of two points higher on the exam (average score of 23 points) compared to public school students (average score of 21 points).[5] SAT results show the average homeschooled student's score is 80 points higher than the average public school student.

These are standardized tests, not content-specific tests, because they need to accommodate a wide range of academic curricula.

The truth hardly anyone in education talks about is that the ACT and SAT are logic and reasoning-based tests. You can get a perfect score on the science section of the ACT and not know a lick of science.

Guess who is proficient at critical thinking, logic, and reasoning?

Homeschoolers. This may be one of the strongest reasons why homeschooling is rising: more families want their kids to develop critical thinking. In fact, classical education places a strong emphasis on logic through high school, a skill that is *essential* for getting strong scores on the ACT and SAT.

While these exams hold significance, they do not define one's entire academic prowess or intelligence. Each individual approaches tests uniquely, and it's within your control to understand your child's learning style and determine the importance you assign to any highly regarded standardized test. However, it's also crucial to acknowledge that colleges award acceptance and scholarships based on standardized test scores. Viewing these tests as opportunities for advancement rather than philosophical avoid-at-all-costs impositions might unlock schools and resources that would not have been available to your student otherwise.

Myth: "Homeschooled High School Students Need an Accredited Diploma to Get into College"

The key word is *accredited*. What does it mean to have accreditation? It is the belief that a peer-conducted review of a specific study, program, or body of work needs to measure against a standard of excellence. The challenge with and freedom of homeschool accreditation is there are few, if any true accreditation standards that are not subject to the whims and shifting influences of the traditional school system.

Thankfully, the question of accreditation is made moot due to the standard acceptance of SAT and ACT tests for aspiring college students. Most colleges and universities accept your child's ACT/SAT score with either an automated transcript or portfolio transcript where you manually compile their list of subjects studied during high school.

Homeschooled students are increasingly being actively recruited by colleges and universities, institutions that are keenly aware of the academic excellence of homeschooled students. Harvard shared this perspective in its admissions process:

> "Standardized tests provide a rough yardstick of what a student has learned over time and how that student might perform academically in college—but they are only one of many factors considered in our admissions process. High school grades can also help assess readiness for college courses, but secondary schools around the country and the world employ a wide variety of grading systems—and some students have no grades at all from their schools or are home-schooled. There is no

'one-size-fits-all' rule about which curriculum to study during secondary school years."[6]

So, don't fall for the accredited diploma myth—it's not absolutely necessary. As demonstrated by the statement from the Harvard University Admissions Counselor, colleges understand that accredited diplomas cannot be solely depended on as foolproof indicators of a student's intellectual ability. This is because the standards used to create these diplomas can vary significantly.

Also, many homeschoolers take advantage of their academic freedom to participate in dual enrollment programs, which allow high schoolers to take college-level courses while still in high school, earning both high school and college credits simultaneously. Dual enrollment provides homeschool students with various benefits, such as the chance to engage in college-level studies, acquire college credits, and potentially reduce the time and cost of their future college education.

> *Homeschooled students are increasingly being actively recruited by colleges and universities.*

If you are considering college for your student, know the alternative measures for academic readiness that exist, and which ones your target colleges will use so your student can prepare accordingly.

Remember This

- Homeschooled students stand above their traditional school peers academically, and colleges are actively recruiting them.

- Having a child with a learning disability is a reason to homeschool, not a reason to put them in the system.

- Trusting experts is important, but no one knows your child better than you.

- Homeschooling multiple children just requires good planning. Many subjects can be taught together, and one can learn everything they need in half the time (or less) than the seven-hour traditional school day.

CHAPTER NINE

Moving Beyond the Shadow of Doubt: Common Homeschooling Hang-Ups and Fears

"When the whole world is running towards a cliff, he who is running in the opposite direction appears to have lost his mind."

—Unknown

Twins. One in each arm, my husband, Scott, beaming with pride, and my mother eager to gobble up our newest little bundles. Those first few ~~days weeks~~ months were a blur. I vividly remember holding one of my twins and telling my mom, "This is too many babies!" And in her loving, trusting way, as only a mom can do, she said, "No, it's just the right amount," and slid my other twin into my arms. Overwhelming, yes. Impossible to figure out, no, there are few things in life that are truly impossible.

Homeschooling may *seem* like an impossible task for you right now.

Maybe you're already feeling overwhelmed, buried under dishes, cleaning up the same toys for the sixth time today, and sighing at the small Mount Everest of clean laundry mocking you from the half-open dryer. I *feel* all of that with you. It's easy to be overwhelmed staring at all of those tasks, especially if you're not getting the support you need to thrive, which is another topic for another time. Is it crazy to think you can homeschool if life already feels like you're drowning?

No, it's not crazy, and I'm willing to bet you're doing better than you're giving yourself credit for today. So, let's sit here in this pile of unfolded, maybe still-clean laundry and talk about courage.

Because what you're thinking about takes *tremendous* courage! Don't let anyone tell you otherwise because nurturing your child's love of learning, introducing them to amazing ideas and subjects, and being there every step of the way is a brave, *brave* adventure.

How do you know you have what it takes? How do you know you can be confident enough to thrive as a homeschooling parent? Maybe most importantly, how can we help shift your mindset from just hoping you don't mess up your child for life to a strong, quiet confidence that you are *the best* teacher for your child?

Embrace the truth that no one on Earth can be a better teacher for your child than you. You don't have to have all the answers.

Embrace the truth that no one on Earth can be a better teacher for your child than you. Your child is looking to you to lead them in their education. No, you don't have to have all the answers. No, you don't have to be the only one teaching your child. What you do need to be is the one taking the brave step to try, to even fail in certain ways, to learn from what does or doesn't work, and to courageously keep pressing on, growing every day.

And along the journey, you'll face your own obstacles, even mental villains, in some cases, that will lie to you. These are insecurities, uncertainties, and even toxic tendencies that can stand in the way of your child learning with the best possible experience. But I promise you, facing these challenges head-on can have beautiful rewards.

It takes having the courage to bust through these myths. Let's start with the first one. It's a biggie . . .

Myth: "Homeschoolers Are Stuck at Home"

There is nothing further from the truth. Homeschoolers participate in myriad activities, clubs, co-ops, enrichments, sports, and extracurricular activities. Seriously, homeschooling your child will open up your *entire* calendar, not just your "after-school" hours.

Where do we get this myth? I suspect it comes from the false idea of having to emulate the school system's seven-hour day at home, then followed by two to three hours more of homework.

Homeschooled children enjoy diverse real-world experiences with people of different backgrounds and ages.

It's not just the myth of homeschoolers huddled around their kitchen table or in the spare bedroom/"classroom" that we need to debunk. I've met homeschoolers at airport gates, coffee shops, community centers, libraries, co-working spaces, and outdoor venues.

What are they doing? Working on a lesson or project surrounded by other remote workers, laptop warriors, and entrepreneurs.

Which also testifies to the next myth on our list.

Myth: "Homeschooled Kids Are Sheltered from the Real World"

False. Critics say our kids won't be ready for the real world because they are sheltered. Yet multiple studies show homeschooled children enjoy a wide range of diverse real-world experiences, including sports, music, theater, and community service, and they interact with a wide variety of people with different backgrounds and ages.[1] What they are sheltered from is the abuse, maltreatment, and conforming social environment created by the traditional school system.

Myth: "Kids Need to Be in School to 'Toughen Up'"

False. This one makes me sad because it implies kids must endure pain to be prepared for the "real world." Yes, the toughness that correlates to success in life is resilience. However, the American Psychological Association recommends building resilience by focusing on these four principles:

- Connection: Build relationships with trustworthy and compassionate people such as family, friends, civic groups, and faith-based communities.

- Wellness: Practice a positive lifestyle, such as proper nutrition, sleep, hydration, and exercise. Practice mindfulness, meaning you are focusing on the present moment.

- Healthy thinking: Maintain hopefulness.

- Meaning: Do something each day that gives you a sense of accomplishment and meaning.[2]

The Mayo Clinic maintains a similar list.[3] Simply look at each preceding practice and ask yourself this: is resilience better developed in a traditional school or through homeschooling? If it means my child *must* be traumatized to learn how life works in the "fast lane," I'm choosing to gently nurture my kids toward resilience without them needing therapy down the road.

Myth: "Homeschooled Kids Will Miss Out on Prom, Team Sports, Clubs, Graduation, and So On"

Nope! With planning, your homeschooler can have as many, and even more, opportunities as a traditional school environment allows. Many local groups host proms, all sorts of ceremonies, and banquets. In fact, many state homeschool organizations host large events such as large-scale graduation ceremonies if that's your kid's preference.

For sports, there are national and regional sports associations for either homeschoolers or everyone, such as local homeschool sports leagues, church-sponsored leagues, YMCA leagues, and so on. Plus, some states have equal access laws, where homeschoolers can try out for public and private sports teams.[4] Also, homeschoolers have access to sports classes during the day, which are often less crowded than evening classes.

> *Homeschoolers access daytime sports, often less crowded than evening ones.*

I've known homeschoolers who were homeschooling *because of* sports. I once knew a homeschool family that homeschooled so they could travel for golf; and we homeschooled, at our learning center, a competitive surfer and also an ice skater.

You may or may not have access to the sports programs at your local public school, but that's worth exploring. However, private schools often are open to homeschoolers and will allow homeschooled students to play on their sports teams if they are enrolled in a class. My friend's son is enrolled in a weightlifting class at a local private high school so he can play on the football team.

In the realm of homeschooling, it's easy to fall into a scarcity mindset, fixating on the idea that our children might miss out on the quintessential American school experience. However, this perspective is limiting, and can blind us to the abundance of unique, additional opportunities that homeschooling provides. While your

> *Fear of children missing the quintessential American school experience can blind us to the abundance of opportunities homeschooling provides.*

child may not attend prom or engage in activities akin to the classic school experience (though many homeschool proms exist for homeschoolers, as do team sports), consider the exceptional possibilities uniquely available to them as homeschoolers. For instance, my own kids have relished the adventure of vacation schooling and have cultivated friendships around the world thanks to homeschooling. Instead of dwelling on what they might not experience conventionally, let's celebrate the incomparable journey they're on. And it truly is incomparable. That, in itself, is special.

Myth: "Kids Who Have a High Social Need Should Not Be Homeschooled"

False. Studies show homeschooling families provide more opportunities for their children to interact and socialize with children and adults in a variety of ways. Homeschooling provides a much richer range and depth of social interactions and experiences than what's available in a traditional classroom. This includes co-ops, community groups, morning or afternoon field trips to museums, concerts, events, shows, community groups, sports, and other extracurricular activities.

The flexibility of homeschooling allows custom tailoring of studies and the environment to the specific needs and interests of the student. This includes adjusting the curriculum and activities to serve students with a higher need for social interactions. Both introverted kids and extroverted kids are a fit for homeschooling.

Myth: "Homeschooled Kids Will Fall behind Academically"

Even though we covered this quite a bit previously, it's important to share some data that will help your confidence as a homeschooling parent. *Developmental Psychology* published findings from N. E. Hill and D. F. Tyson show that there are over 50 independent studies proving a strong correlation between student academic success and family involvement; with no perceived variance due to the family's socio-economic status or the perceived academic prestige of their particular school.[5] Simply being more involved in your child's learning is a proven factor in their future academic success.

There's one crucial detail to note about all the statistics we've covered regarding homeschoolers' academic performance. To the best of my understanding, none of the quoted studies comparing homeschoolers' academic progress versus traditionally schooled students segment the homeschooled students' results by homeschooling type. I have not seen any documented delineation of academic results specific to Charlotte Mason, Unit Study, Interest-Led, Unschooling, or any other subsegment of homeschoolers.

It's not that one home-schooling type is better—homeschooling is simply better academically, period.

What does that tell us? It's not that any single one homeschooling type is better than the rest—it's that homeschooling is simply better academically, period.

Fear: "I Don't Have the Expertise and Knowledge of the Subject Matter to Teach My Kids"

"But, Christy, what if the subjects or concepts are too advanced for me?!" Here's what our friends who are unfamiliar with the homeschool culture don't understand: homeschooling is largely about sourcing. If you have an advanced subject you don't feel comfortable or

Sourcing is your superpower.

equipped to tackle yourself, you can outsource that subject to a more qualified instructor who fits your child's needs and aligns with your family's way of homeschooling. In fact, there are world-class instructors who specialize in topics and are readily available to teach your child in each subject.

As your child gets older and the topics more specialized, sourcing is a true superpower for you to give your child the most customized learning experience that children in traditional school settings can only *dream* of receiving. You can purchase scripted curriculum with video lessons, find online classes (both live and self-paced), and sample so many flavors of in-person or virtual classes.

I wish every child could be educated with that level of personalization.

Fear: "I Don't Have the Patience to Homeschool"

There are two myths we need to address here.

The first myth is that homeschooling parents have more patience than non-homeschooling parents. I can verify this is simply not true. Secondly, it's important to understand that patience is not an immutable trait, but rather a skill that can be developed and nurtured. So, the answer to the question "Do I have the patience to homeschool?" lies in an internal conversation with yourself.

I did not just shout into the universe one day that we were homeschooling and the three spirits of Charlotte Mason, John Taylor Gatto, and Mother Theresa bestowed on me a supernatural gift of extraordinary patience as unit studies rained down on me from on high. That didn't happen. Funny to imagine, yes, but simply not true.

I am just as patient (or more accurately, impatient) as essentially any other parent. Hopefully, it's more patience than my kids need, but there are some days . . .

But this is what I've learned. In the intricate journey of parenting, it's essential to recognize that patience is not a fixed trait, bestowed upon us at birth and unchangeable thereafter. Instead, it's a virtue that can be nurtured and developed, much like a skill honed over time. This understanding is pivotal because, regardless of whether you homeschool or not, with increased patience, not only does one's own quality of life improve, but the bonds within the family grow stronger, creating a more harmonious household.

Yet, it's completely normal for parents to find themselves at their wit's end.

There are moments when the prospect of spending even more time with your children feels overwhelming. It's in these instances that the thought may arise, "If I homeschool, is this what a whole day of homeschooling would be like?" The answer? "Perhaps." If one genuinely feels that patience is an area where growth is not desired or seems unattainable, it's important to acknowledge that homeschooling might present challenges.

However, it's worth considering that homeschooling offers a unique advantage—the ability to customize the learning environment to cater to your child's distinct needs and learning style. This tailored approach can lead to a more seamless and productive learning experience. In turn, this can alleviate some of the frustrations that might necessitate a surplus of patience.

Moreover, it's crucial to understand that exercising patience in homeschooling doesn't imply a constant state of boundless endurance. Realistic expectations, intermittent breaks, self-regulation, and the discovery of methods that resonate with both you and your child play a significant role in managing any moments of impatience that may arise.

Ultimately, the journey of parenting and homeschooling is an evolving process. It's about recognizing our capacities for patience, understanding that they can grow, and finding strategies to navigate this path with grace.

Through this, we not only foster our children's development but also embark on a personal journey of growth and self-discovery.

Fear: "I Can't Homeschool because My Kid Won't Listen to Me"

It may not be that you're concerned about having enough patience to homeschool, but rather whether or not your child will listen to you when it comes to homeschooling.

If you're grappling with concerns about whether your child will listen to you in the homeschooling journey, you may find yourself in one of two common camps. First, there's the worry about stepping into the "teacher role" and whether your child will respect your authority in this new dynamic. In the later sections of this book, you'll find an encouraging chapter on deschooling, which addresses this very concern. A question that frequently arises is, "How do you switch between being a teacher and a mom?" The answer is surprisingly simple—you don't. Just like when you taught your child to eat or walk, you didn't switch hats; you were always their guide and nurturer. This is the essence of homeschooling: a seamless blend of natural learning within the family dynamic.

During deschooling, you and your child recalibrate your understanding of learning and teaching, shedding preconceived notions about traditional education. This phase fosters an environment where mutual respect, trust, and effective communication can thrive. It's not about wearing multiple hats but about cultivating a rich, integrated learning experience.

Homeschooling is not about wearing multiple hats at different times of the day but about a lifestyle of seamlessly blending learning into your family culture.

The second camp has more to do with parenting in general. If you are worried your child won't listen to you, remember that this issue isn't exclusive to homeschooling. Effective communication and mutual respect are vital in any parent-child relationship. Whether homeschooling or not, persistently ignoring parental guidance can lead to challenges such as strained relationships, hindered learning, safety risks, and hindered social and emotional development. It's crucial for parents to work on fostering these skills in a loving way. Consider parenting classes, seminars, or books to enhance your family dynamic and support your child's growth.

Homeschooling, particularly for those with a growth mindset, can offer incredible rewards. Personally, I started therapy a few years ago to work on some of my "stuff." This journey helped me recognize areas in which I could improve as a spouse and parent, providing me with valuable tools.

I truly believe in my heart that one of the most significant factors contributing to a fulfilling homeschooling experience is the willingness to address personal growth, which extends beyond homeschooling to parenting in general. If we're committed to becoming better versions of ourselves for our families, we are happier people and homeschooling becomes more enjoyable.

When I make a conscious effort to do constant, meaningful work on who I am as a person, a wife, and as a parent, the results are so worth it. I constantly need to keep working on how I show up in different areas of life and situations.

This means taking classes, having tough conversations, looking inward, being vulnerable, apologizing when needed, reading more books, and always remaining open to learning and growth.

Fear: "What If My Child Doesn't Want to Homeschool?"

A lot of kids don't want to homeschool, especially children who are about to be pulled out of traditional schooling. "Mom, I'm going to lose all of my friends!" "I don't want to be the weird kid doing school at home." "I don't want you to be my teacher. You don't know how to teach!"

It's natural to be afraid of the unknown. It's the same reason why we don't want to walk into just any dark room. What if we don't like what we find?

This is a great time for you to ask yourself, "What is *best* for your child? What is *best* for your family?" A while back, I interviewed a panel of adults who were homeschooled, ranging from all walks of life and homeschooling types. One of the men shared that he *hated* the idea of homeschooling, but his mom knew it was the right decision for him and their family. She stayed strong, sticking to what she *knew* was right for them, and today he's incredibly thankful he was homeschooled.

I also find Amy's story interesting. She was classically homeschooled . . . and (you may be seeing the theme here) she hated it. Amy didn't like that her parents chose to stick with it, but after graduation, she attended a highly prestigious university. What did she discover upon arriving? Her homeschooling background taught her how to study and learn with a truly proficient mind. While the other freshmen panicked, not knowing how to accomplish all that was put on their plate, Amy knew exactly how to tackle the academic demands of a rigorous university.

This is not unusual. Other parents have related similar experiences when their kids enter the military, college, even building their own business.

As for Amy? She's brilliant and is now a world-class instructor on a complex subject. The best part is that she now thanks her parents for making the tough decision and doing what was best for her and her family.

Your child may complain or do homeschooling kicking and screaming for a while. One of my friends who pulled her older kids out of the school system told me her kids complained for the entire first year. But now? They are thankful they are homeschooled. She stood strong, was the loving leader, and did what was right for her family.

Remember this fact: your child isn't grown up yet, so it's unreasonable to expect them to always know what's best for their future. Kids almost always know what they want, but they don't always know what they need. That's why being a loving parent leader is so important. It's our job to assess, to the best of our ability, what our children need, while still making sure they are seen and heard.

Kids almost always know what they want, but they don't always know what they need.

Planning their future together is a wonderful, shared experience, but ultimately, the main responsibility lies with you. While involving our children in decisions, we also understand the significance of teaching and modeling effective decision-making skills. It's important to acknowledge that, due to our life experiences and broader perspective, we often have insights that they may not grasp yet. Our choices are guided by a deep love and concern for their well-being, even if they may not fully appreciate it at this moment. Remember, when children know they are cherished and that your decisions are rooted in their best interests, they'll find it easier to accept choices they may not initially like. This sets the foundation for mutual respect and trust in the family dynamic.

Fear: "How Can I Teach If I'm Not Certified or Credentialed?"

A 2015 study by Brian Ray shows homeschooled students score on average 30 percentile points higher than traditional school students on standardized tests.[6] There was no significant difference in test results for students whose parents were trained educators versus those whose parents were not trained educators.

As a now-former teacher and someone who worked closely with teachers at all levels of education for 20 years, I can tell you much of teaching is about sourcing your material. Teachers in the traditional school system often are using a curriculum that in many cases provides activities, discussion questions, assignments, and assessments. If you know someone who is a teacher in a traditional school setting, you've probably heard them talk about lesson planning. What they're referring to is planning out the time ahead, knowing the material you will cover, and understanding what objectives, activities, projects, and assignments you will be doing.

The good news is that much, if not all of the curricula used inside traditional schools, including private schools, are readily available to homeschoolers too. You can read from the exact same pages of the same textbooks or teacher's guides. You can watch the same pre-recorded videos, use the same online programs, and follow the same steps to complete assignments and projects as virtually any other teacher in your area if you're so inclined.

When you homeschool, if you want to outsource a topic, especially an advanced topic, you have the power to hand-select the teacher you want to teach your child. That's the power of sourcing and being the general contractor for building your child's education.

Fear: "What If My Partner Won't Support My Decision to Homeschool?"

I come across this question quite frequently, and it's a complex situation to navigate. If you find yourself facing a lack of support from your partner regarding homeschooling, it's important to consider the overall health of your relationship first. If there are underlying issues or unresolved conflicts, addressing those should take priority over discussions about your child's education. I am not a licensed marriage counselor or therapist, so it's best to seek professional guidance in such circumstances.

Navigating the quandary where one spouse wants to homeschool while the other does not can be challenging. Here are some suggestions for a step-by-step process to address this situation:

1. Open and Honest Communication: Start by having open and honest conversations with your spouse about your desire to homeschool. Listen to their concerns and make an effort to understand their perspective.

2. Educate Yourself: Research and gather information about homeschooling, its benefits, and success stories. Present factual data and reliable resources to help your spouse gain a better understanding of homeschooling.

3. Address Concerns: Take the time to address any concerns your spouse may have. Listen empathetically

and provide reassurance where possible. Be prepared to compromise and find common ground to alleviate their worries.

4. Seek Professional Guidance: Consider consulting with a licensed marriage counselor or family therapist who can help facilitate constructive discussions and provide guidance tailored to your specific situation.

5. Explore Co-op or Hybrid Options: Propose the idea of enrolling your child in a homeschool co-op or hybrid program. These options can provide a compromise by combining elements of homeschooling and traditional schooling, addressing both educational and social concerns.

6. Trial Period: Suggest a trial period for homeschooling, during which you can assess its effectiveness and impact on your child's education and overall family dynamics. Reassure your spouse that you are willing to reassess and make adjustments if needed.

7. Showcase Homeschooling Benefits: Show your spouse examples of successful homeschooling stories and highlight the flexibility, personalized learning, and individualized attention that homeschooling can offer.

8. Involve Your Partner: Encourage your spouse to actively participate in your child's education, even if they are not directly homeschooling. Involve them in lesson planning, educational activities, and field trips to foster a sense of shared involvement.

9. Seek Support: Connect with other homeschooling families or support groups to demonstrate that

homeschooling is a viable and supported educational choice. Encourage your spouse to engage with these communities to gain a broader perspective.

10. Revisit the Decision: Regularly revisit and reassess the decision to homeschool as a family. Evaluate the progress, challenges, and overall satisfaction of both you and your spouse. Remain open to adjusting your approach or exploring alternative educational options if necessary.

Remember, finding a solution that works for both partners requires patience, understanding, and compromise. It's essential to prioritize the well-being and educational needs of your child while fostering a healthy relationship with your spouse.

Fear: "What If My Relatives and Friends Won't Support My Decision to Homeschool?"

When navigating the challenge of unsupportive friends or relatives regarding your decision to homeschool, it's important to approach the situation with empathy, kindness, and a willingness to set healthy boundaries. Begin by recognizing that each person may have their own perspectives and concerns, and it's crucial to respect their viewpoints, even if you disagree. Remember that your choice to homeschool is based on what you believe is best for your family and your children's education.

As you engage in conversations, mentally categorize individuals into two groups: those who are open-minded, eager to learn, and genuinely interested in understanding your reasons for homeschooling, and those who are more resistant to change and may be firmly set in their ways.

For those in the first group, engage in open and honest discussions, sharing your experiences, research, and the benefits you see in homeschooling. Encourage them to ask questions, express their concerns, and have a genuine dialogue that fosters mutual understanding. It could very well be that before you know it, your concerned loved one, newly equipped with accurate information, answers, and data, will transform into one of your biggest homeschool cheerleaders.

Your family's educational journey should be rooted in your belief in its positive impact on your family.

However, there may be individuals in the second group who are less inclined to embrace alternative perspectives. In such cases, it's important to set boundaries and agree to disagree. Recognize that not everyone will fully understand or support your decision, and that's okay. Focus on maintaining a respectful relationship while gently asserting your commitment to homeschooling and your belief in its positive impact on your family.

Over time, you will naturally discover which individuals are open to personal growth and learning, and which ones may be more resistant. Be patient and open-minded, as people can evolve and change their perspectives with time. Nurture the relationships where growth and understanding are possible, and gracefully accept that some individuals may never fully embrace your homeschooling choice. Ultimately, your commitment to your family's educational journey should be rooted in love, compassion, and a desire to provide the best learning environment for your children.

Fear: "I'm So Scared of Being Lonely. I Don't Want to Be Miserable"

When your child is in the traditional school system, you as a parent or caregiver automatically have a built-in social structure. This is one of the biggest challenges I help homeschooling parents and caregivers overcome: "Christy, I don't want to feel all alone!" A lot of the confusion and in some cases antagonism toward homeschooling from other parents and caregivers is not knowing if they could make the same brave decision as you are. Homeschooling isn't for everyone—and that's okay.

When you decide to homeschool your child, your landscape of friends *is going* to change! It takes some time because yes, homeschooling your child is a social sacrifice at first (let me emphasize *at first*). You, as an adult, don't have as much freedom or flexibility in your schedule. It's *so* much harder to grab lunch with friends at that chic new restaurant when your child is with you or if it means getting behind on lessons.

Please invest in finding your homeschool community. We have a welcoming, fun community in my Thrive membership group that is great for homeschooling parents and caregivers to receive expert homeschool academic advice, unwavering support, and a place to truly belong. But mine is not the only one; there are a plethora of great communities that can help you know you're doing well and help you figure out this whole homeschooling thing. You don't have to wait to find your people, we are already here, waiting for you.

But can we talk about this idea of loneliness? Seasons of loneliness can be gifts, and our collective society tends to always see loneliness as a discomfort to be avoided. When you lean into that discomfort, loneliness can be a conduit for growth.

Invest in finding your homeschool community. They are already waiting for you.

Fatima relocated across states, leaving her circle of great friends and homeschooling families, and for the first few months, she felt incredibly lonely. Fatima had a choice: stay in this loneliness, in hopes of it eventually being replaced by new friends, or lean into this season as a way to grow closer with her daughter, her husband, and their family. Ultimately, as time went on, Fatima found that community did emerge. She forged meaningful connections and lasting friendships, solidifying her sense of belonging in their new home. Looking back, she treasures the way she used that period of solitude as a catalyst for growth and the foundation of cherished relationships. Friends and community did come, but she made the most out of her time.

Gray Cardinals

One day, as I was getting ready, my eight-year-old daughter surprised me by joining me on the bed with a sticker-by-number book about birds. She wanted to spend time together while I did my makeup, working on a page of a cardinal.

As I glanced over, I noticed she was sticking brown stickers instead of red ones, and I playfully pointed out that she had chosen a different bird. To my surprise, she looked at me with a wise expression and said, "Mommy, this is a female cardinal. Only the males are red."

Intrigued, I asked her to explain the reason behind the color difference. She went on to tell me that the males were red to attract attention and establish dominance, while the females were brown for camouflage to protect their nests and eggs. But what struck me most was her genuine admiration for the females, as she believed they had the most important and exciting role in the world. At that moment, I realized the profound lesson hidden in her innocent explanation.

Choosing to homeschool is not always the easiest path. I understand the allure of pursuing a career, enjoying lunch dates with friends, and having the freedom to travel and chase professional opportunities. As a parent, you may wonder if the sacrifices made to homeschool your child are worth it. It can sometimes feel like your partner has the spotlight, with a successful career and societal validation, while you remain in the background.

Let me assure you: You are far from invisible. By choosing to homeschool, you have the privilege of nurturing and shaping your child into a remarkable individual who can make a positive impact on the world. They may go on to achieve great things, garnering admiration and recognition. Or they may find fulfillment and purpose in the quiet joys of building their own family. Your role as a homeschooling parent is invaluable, and the impact you have on your child's life is immeasurable.

Cherish the journey of homeschooling; you are investing in something truly extraordinary.

As tears welled up in my eyes, my daughter's voice brimming with excitement, I couldn't help but feel a profound sense of gratitude for the lessons she taught me that day. While there may be moments when you yearn for a more independent, career-driven life, remember that your choice to prioritize your child's education and well-being is one filled with love and purpose. Cherish the journey of homeschooling, knowing that you are investing in something truly extraordinary.

Remember This

- As your child's homeschooling parent or caregiver, you are far more competent and committed to your child's education than any other teacher you could find.

- It's normal to have uncertainty about homeschooling. Remember nervously learning to drive and looking in five dozen different directions? And look how you drive now! Eventually, homeschooling becomes second nature too.

- Choosing to homeschool isn't the easiest path. But it is incredibly rewarding. You can curate the family life, childhoods, and education that you want for your family.

Finding Your Why and Leaning into Hope

CHAPTER TEN

Deschooling: Your Bridge over Anxious Waters

"They check in on you, right? To make sure you are doing
everything correctly?"

—Quote to me from a retired teacher regarding
government supervision of my homeschool

We've seen what the data and studies tell us: the traditional
schooling system is deteriorating all aspects of our children's health, well-being, love of learning, and key relationships in our homes. This is a toxic environment, and if left
unchecked, it will cause untold damage for generations.

Your child is at risk, but they're not the only one in danger. As a parent, do you love school more or less than when
you attended school? There's a good chance you don't feel
as positive about school *because* of what school has done to
your child.

You've likely heard the story that if you put a frog in
water and slowly turn up the heat, it will stay there being
comfortable, unaware of its peril, until it boils to death.
Despite it being not correct (they will try to jump out),[1] it's
a great metaphor for what happens to us when we're raised
in the traditional school system. It's easy not to realize the

true danger of staying there until we're past the boiling point: lethargy of interest in learning, a severe change in all aspects of health, a disorientation about what is true or not, and if left untreated, death of joy and well-being.

We need to be the frogs that leap out of the heating water pot. Only when we get far enough out of the system, and void of any vested interest in its perpetuation, can we look back and see the bigger and clearer picture.

It's not our fault if no one told us this before now. We grew up thinking whatever we experienced in the traditional school system was how learning was done. Through no fault of ours, this is the belief we bought without question. We grew up in this system. We trusted this system. But now, how do we break from this system?

You've considered all the factors and made the decision to homeschool.

And yet, there is a natural sense of doubt. Can the *unknown* of homeschooling be noticeably better than the *known* dangers of the traditional school system? When I talk with parents who make the brave decision to homeschool their children, I hear their doubt and uncertainty, and see it in their eyes:

> *"I still can't believe homeschooling could give my child everything our school does. I mean, our staff has won so many awards and we're in a really great district."*

> *"How do I make sure my kid is learning all that he is supposed to?"*

> *"What about high school? I can't teach all those advanced subjects . . ."*

> *"What about Friday night lights and prom?"*

So, let's address this reality.

Deschooling Is Essential for Detoxifying

You've been programmed.

And if your child has spent much time in the school system, they've been programmed too.

A more accurate description would be "imprinted." The reason it's difficult to get free of school system preferences is not because of "conditioning." It's because of "imprinting." And to give you and your child the best homeschool experience, the best practice is to overwrite this imprinting with a healthier one.

Imprinting is a subconscious learning by attachment; a narrowing of ones preferences and beliefs as a result of initial exposure to something. The imprinting most of us are familiar with is *filial* imprinting such as ducklings following their mother.[2] More interesting for our purposes here is that imprinting can occur not just to living things, but to inanimate, non-living things also.

Peregrine falcons imprint on specific structures for their breeding grounds, and a number of well-known studies show birds attaching themselves to boots and other objects.[3] For our corner of the animal kingdom, *homo humanus* (i.e., us), we likewise imprint on both people and inanimate objects. Of prime interest to deschooling are organizational imprinting and Baby Duck Syndrome.[4,5]

Organizational imprinting means that we tend to prefer organizational structures that we were initially

The reason it's difficult to get free of school system preferences is not because of its "conditioning." It's because of its "imprinting."

exposed to. On the other hand, Baby Duck Syndrome describes our tendency to develop a strong preference for the first type of something we encounter, and subsequently view different types as less desirable. PC or Mac? Style of silverware? School system or . . . you get the picture.

"But Christy, isn't this the same as conditioning?"

You may be thinking of *Pavlovian conditioning,*[6] where, for example, Ivan Pavlov famously got a dog to associate a bell ringing with being fed, and then salivating. Got him the Nobel Prize.

There's a difference, and it is crucial. Conditioning is learning by association at any point in time. Imprinting, on the other hand, is learning by attachment, on initial relationship. And key, as you can see from Baby Duck Syndrome, conditioning is learned subconscious *behavior,* but imprinting is learned subconscious *belief,* which is why it is so difficult to undo; *belief* is much harder to change than *behavior.*

Conditioning is learned behavior. Imprinting is learned belief and is much harder to change.

In further response to your question, in addition to being imprinted by the system, yes, we've also been conditioned by it to behave in certain ways. Raise our hand to go to the bathroom, keep quiet, and . . . the bell rings . . . "Quick, quick! To the next room!" We dutifully change rooms, sit down, wag our tails, and wait for our next helping of school. Pavlov? Nothing compared to the school system.

Yet it is the imprinting that is much more of a challenge to unravel. Where conditioning might be the bell and food bowl, imprinting is the collar and leash. And now that we've chosen to get out of that collar, we don't want to subconsciously put it right back on our kids. Keeping with the metaphor, we need to remove that collar stitch by stitch, until it literally just falls off us. That's deschooling.

Without engaging in the process of deschooling, we risk inadvertently constructing the very same confines that we sought to escape.

Breaking away from the tradi-tional school system can be liberat-ing, yet it's astonishing how deeply persistent these ingrained restrictive habits and beliefs can be; similar to how animals can keep behaviors they learned in captivity even after being

> *Without engaging in deschooling we risk constructing the very same confines we sought to escape.*

released back into the wild. This imprinting, this prison of the mind, and what has become ingrained in our world-view, is far harder to escape than the traditional school sys-tem itself. Yeonmi Park's experience, referenced earlier in Chapter 3, can help guide us here also:

> "It's not easy to give up a worldview that is built into your bones and imprinted on your brain like the sound of your own father's voice."[7]

Deschooling is the way we get through this maelstrom. Think of deschooling not as rejecting the traditional system. Think of it as simply putting one system of education behind us and moving on in the direction of a better one; replacing one that causes harm and disorientation to our children with one that can impart joy and well-being. And in the process, foster a purposeful and forceful sense of optimism and liberation.

Deschooling is, in a sense, detoxifying the mind. In considering deschooling, we can learn much from the health industry. For many situations, whether it's addiction

Think of deschooling not as rejecting the traditional school system, but simply setting it behind us and moving on in the direction of a better one.

recovery, healing from a traumatic experience, or even healing from surgery, the journey of therapy is not the goal. Health and restoration are the desired outcome, but where many addicts, patients, and clinical guests fall short of their goal is treating the journey of therapy as the goal, not the bridge to reach their goal.

Deschooling Initiates Clarity and Reconstruction of Thought

Working to remove the toxic habits and practices that were imprinted and conditioned is not enough. To avoid a relapse, we must replace them with healthy ones.

If your diet is primarily junk food, it's easy to believe *not* eating junk food will curb its effect. However, a much healthier, more sustainable habit is to replace junk food with nutritious meals and snacks. If negative habits are not replaced with restorative, healthier habits, the end goal is missed. In fact, the regression into the same unhealthy habits can be much worse than before.

This is why so many weight loss experiences are "yo-yo" diets—losing weight, regaining the same weight, if not more, and the cycle repeats. Removing without replacing creates a vacuum of unhealthy habits waiting to return. In deschooling, therefore, we don't just remove the "schooling," but rather, one piece at a time, we replace our society's traditional school paradigms with more healthy and personalized homeschool ones.

The second way deschooling (and homeschooling in general) helps us is in reconstructing our thinking, restoring clarity and confidence in how we think. The modern-day classroom is increasingly teaching students not how to think, but what to think. When we extricate our kids from this environment, they gain a new clarity as they learn to think and reason for themselves and make sense or (nonsense) of what is presented to them. Likewise, so do us parents, as we get increased separation from that system.

It's having that quiet confidence to know *why* you believe the way you do.

It's the ability to engage with complex concepts and even controversial topics using your mind and opinion with greater clarity than ever before. It's the freedom in knowing *you* are in charge of your family's future. You *don't* have to assume anyone else's belief system or agenda.

In deschooling, we don't remove the "schooling," but overwrite the imprinted traditional school paradigms, one small piece at a time, with healthier and personalized homeschool ones.

In deschooling, we do a slow, intentional piece-by-piece rebuilding of how you and your child learn. As Augustine would say, we are ordering or re-ordering the loves. Subject by subject, it's a methodical reintegration of learning in the context of education. When you're ready to end deschooling and start homeschooling, you will have the confidence and clarity you need to thrive.

This is about empowering your mind to speak, act, and respond without feeling belittled or unqualified because you don't hold a certain set of credentials. It's also the tantalizing truth that you are now awake to what's happening in the world of education. You escaped the system. You're free! Create the life you desperately crave with the people you cherish more than anything in the world!

You already have all the permission you need. This is your life. Cross over the bridge of deschooling and I promise, you will reach an extraordinary world wiser, braver, and more fulfilled than you could ever imagine.

Deschooling Helps to Level the Storm

It's not unusual for homeschoolers to get dismayed when, close to the start of their homeschooling, things get rough.

"This isn't what I expected. Is this what it's going to be like?"

"I never should have tried this. I really haven't got what it takes."

"How can we possibly get through this?"

> *Walk over the bridge of deschooling and I promise, you will reach an extraordinary world wiser, braver, and more fulfilled than you could ever imagine.*

This is okay. It's part of the journey, and one hardly addressed. You're teambuilding! The good news is that it's temporary, and the great news is that deschooling can be a great help to smooth over and even erase these potholes in the road.

We call this challenge that deschooling helps you through "Tuckerman." Your family is going to be transitioning into a team that must work together and push through changing dynamics for you to truly thrive with homeschooling. When you make the decision to homeschool, your family will be forming into a team. No matter how old your children are or how many children you have, you are creating a new identity: you're a homeschooling family. A homeschooling team. And as a new team, you will be coming face to face with the typical dynamics of any new team.

In 1965, psychologist Bruce Tuckman identified several key phases that every group or team goes through as it develops.[8] After a new team forms, and after the initial excitement wears off, members find themselves negotiating their new relationships and boundaries, creating conflict and friction. Tuckerman called this the "Storming" stage.

This is one of the most crucial stages of growth for your new little group, as forward motion slows and can even stop. It's not uncommon for teams, including homeschooling ones, to get hung up in the Storming stage and not survive it.

Deschooling to the rescue. By having a good deschooling plan that gradually introduces your new practices, you can weather the storm and come out stronger, and in many cases, curtail conflict before it can grow.

This is a storm, no question about it, so what's *really* happening?

Boundaries are being tested. Tension and arguments are almost inevitable. Personalities will clash and you will likely find yourself pinching away a migraine while nursing your second bottle um . . . glass of wine. Your child doesn't like the new schedule.

They get a taste of freedom, and in "give them an inch . . ." fashion, push for an unhealthy diet of no parameters or guidelines. Maybe mom or dad was the fun-loving one when the kids were all in school, but now, mom is being called the "bad guy" or the "Killer of Joy and Light and All Good Things Under the Sun." (Yes, children can certainly be creative when they care deeply about an idea.) Or this is where a parent, trying to duplicate traditional school at home, gets frazzled and overloaded by all the work, decides it's not working, and the dream dies.

By the way, when switching from nonhomeschooling to homeschooling, you likely will need to level up your parenting game. But this will only make you a better parent, foster better relationships with your kids, and be well worth it. You may even want to reexamine how you parent your child during your deschooling time because you'll have some good mental and emotional "space" to give it the consideration it's worth.

If you are anything like me, you will need to establish new boundaries with more time around each other. "Mama just needs some *alone* time!" My kids know that when my honkin' noise-canceling headphones are on, that I'm in "Only-Interrupt-in-Case-of-Emergency" mode.

I believe in you. I *know* you're on the "growth plan" because you're already intentional with your child's education. I *know* you'll do what you need to do with your parenting to make this all work well. You've got this.

Caught in a storm right now as you're reading this? Hey, it's me, right here with you in the middle of it. Look around you. You did something *brave* and *beautiful* for your family! I know it's really hard to see through storms a lot of times, but I want you to know something: you're not alone. Maybe that's why you're reading this book, or maybe you're re-reading this section from a few months or a year ago because you weren't in a storm then, but, wow, you're in the storm now. You want to know it's all going to be okay.

Yes, it *will* be okay for one big reason: you love your child more than life itself. You would do anything for your child, including taking a big, messy step like homeschooling. No, your child probably doesn't realize this right now, but this is hard for you, too. They don't see your tears at the end of the day. They don't see you tossing another book aside (hopefully, not this book!) because it didn't give you the answers you're needing right now. They don't feel the doubts, questions, or even the swirling voices in your head lying to you about this choice. And you may be struggling to even read this sentence right now because the tears are blurring your vision.

It's okay. This is all worth it. Unwinding so much of what we *thought* was true about school and learning and loving our kids as they grow is super hard. But it does get easier. It may take longer than you want, but not as long as you may expect.

Deschooling Is Essential for Your Family's Joy and Love of Learning

As Ivan Illich, Austrian philosopher, noted in "Deschooling Society":

> "We have come to realize that for most men the right to learn is curtailed by the obligation to attend school."[9]

So, what exactly *is* deschooling?

From my perspective, deschooling is the deliberate undertaking of shedding toxic beliefs, patterns, actions, and choices that have been imprinted by the traditional school system. Its purpose is to cultivate a healthier mindset about leaving traditional school, enabling you to wholeheartedly embrace the educational path you chose for your family. And if done well, with unwavering confidence.

Deschooling is deliberately shedding toxic beliefs, patterns, actions, and choices that have been imprinted by the traditional school system.

Why is deschooling a process? Because both you and your child are unaccustomed to having a say in education. In the traditional school system, students often follow a collective path and conform to rules that stifle their individuality. Deschooling involves breaking free from this mindset and empowering both you and your child to take charge of the educational journey.

It's a transformative process that allows you, as a parent, to determine your desires and priorities for your child's education, creating a tailored learning experience that aligns with their interests, strengths, and values. Embracing deschooling means stepping into new territory, but it opens doors to endless educational possibilities and personal growth.

Deschooling means stepping into new territory, but it opens doors to endless educational possibilities and personal growth.

Part of the deschooling process is unraveling the layers of indoctrination, conditioning, and that psychological imprinting we discussed earlier, to reclaim your own autonomy, identity, and ability to master critical thinking. How can we reasonably detach from our past experiences and presuppositions about schooling and learning unless we replace them with healthier beliefs about what learning could be?

Deschooling is an acknowledgment that you, your child, and your family are worth a different approach. As Peter Gray eloquently puts it, "There is no love of learning if there is only extrinsic motivation."[10] The traditional school system often makes students believe that learning is laborious, and thus, inherently negative. This framing leads to the perception that learning itself is undesirable.

Deschooling is an acknowledgment that you, your child, and your family are worth a different approach.

But What If I Never Went to Traditional Schools?

Some families who have been homeschooling for years still need to do some deschooling. Even some homeschoolers who never even attended a traditional school. "Christy, how is that possible?" The toxicity of the traditional school system is reinforced in entertainment, cultural expectations (spring break doesn't have to only happen in March), and in the day-to-day conversations we have with neighbors, friends, and family members.

If there's any doubt or uncertainty, let me be clear: If your child has spent any significant amount of time in the system, you *and* your child need to deschool. I know, you're probably already thinking, "Really, Christy? Are you sure?"

The No. 1 sign I see from parents who need to deschool is when they ask me, "Is my child learning what they're supposed to be learning?" Beneath this question lies a deeper implication: the belief that there is a predetermined set of knowledge and skills that all children must acquire based on their age or grade level.

Some families who have been homeschooling for years still need to do some deschooling.

However, this mindset overlooks a more fundamental question: "Why do I feel pressured to prioritize my child learning specific facts, details, and skills based on external expectations?" This reflection is crucial because it reveals the influence of our own educational experiences and societal norms, even if we were previously homeschooled or have been homeschooling for a while. It prompts us to question whether these beliefs truly align with our children's unique learning paths and individual growth.

The No. 1 sign I see from parents who need to deschool is when they ask me, "Is my child learning what they're supposed to be learning?"

The sway of societal norms and the internalized pressure to meet certain expectations can significantly impact our confidence as homeschooling parents. I vividly remember a specific kids' class that laid bare my own insecurities. I found myself urging my children to write their names in cursive, unlike the other kids who were printing. This puzzled me because, truthfully, I hadn't even taught them how to print yet. I feared that if they attempted, it might not turn out as polished as I hoped, leading to potential judgment. But why did it weigh so heavily on me?

Beneath the surface, I was harboring an anxiety that the group leader might scrutinize me if my children didn't excel in printing, despite their exceptional cursive abilities. In that moment, my children's true capabilities were overshadowed by my own self-doubt, fueled by the fear of appearing inadequate. These moments serve as stark reminders of the ongoing journey of deschooling, illustrating that even experienced homeschoolers like myself can still grapple with ingrained beliefs and expectations.

When and How to Deschool

Deschooling is a highly individualized process, taking on a unique form for each family. The damaging effect of traditional school can vary widely and this should be taken into account when planning a deschooling process. The more different a child is than the perceived norm, the greater the chances that they have been maltreated.[11,12] A huge trap I see families fall into during their transition is pulling their kids out of school on a Friday and starting a full-blown all-in-one (read: expensive) curriculum for homeschooling on Monday. That's one of the worst steps any family can take. You *and* your child both likely need an adjustment period, which is exciting (it truly will be so fun!).

When it comes to deschooling, there are different opinions among homeschooling advocates. Some say you should have a deschooling period of one month for every year your child spent in traditional school, and they also may encourage jumping right into an "unschooling" approach, meaning no academics whatsoever unless your child has interest. Following that advice, in my opinion, can cause a lot of anxiety because it's like putting the cart before the horse. Personally, I have a different take.

During the deschooling phase, parents often worry their child will fall behind if they don't immediately start a structured curriculum. It's completely understandable because we're conditioned to believe education must follow a strict timeline and meet specific standards. We still hold ourselves to these expectations, fearing any deviation will hinder our child's progress. Going cold turkey is a formula for panic.

A trap families fall into is pulling kids out of school on Friday and starting full-blown all in one (read: expensive) curriculum the following Monday.

Here's my gentle approach: focus on the basics like reading, writing, and math, while giving plenty of room for exploration and pursuing your child's interests. It's all about finding balance. In regard to how long one should deschool, that is for every family to decide. It's certainly not a week. I'd look at least a month but it's probably best to embrace more, depending on your own progress in deschooling and the time you need to put a homeschooling plan together or adjust your current one.

One of the best pieces of advice I can give you is to *take your time*. Don't microwave your deschooling process. Take the time you need. Enjoy it. That's why I recommend parents continue to focus on the fundamentals during this phase. It ensures you won't feel overwhelmed or pressured to rush through it. Your child will be fine and it's better for you to stand on your own two feet before concluding this phase.

The important part is that you have fun because you're reawakening the love of learning for the entire family. Homeschooling is a life-giving, fun-filled adventure where your kids get to have a say in what they learn and how. There's no right or wrong in this reawakening season. You're now in charge!

My gentle deschooling approach: focus on basics like reading, writing, and math, while giving plenty of room to pursue your child's interests.

One of the most comfortable and realistic ways to deschool is to have a lightly structured schedule and a sensible, compassionate plan to backfill that time in an engaging way. Whatever path you take for your deschooling, I recommend that it include certain intentional activities:

- **Legalize.** Before you remove your child from school, understand and follow your state's legal requirements. There are homeschool organizations and legal experts who specialize in helping families with meeting those requirements.

- **Decompress.** This is going to be a *big* transition for your family, so now may be a perfect time to soak up some rest and relaxation before diving into homeschooling. How about starting off with a vacation? When was the last time your family had a nice trip, not necessarily expensive, but a vacation to a favorite place or doing a favorite activity? Use this time to decompress a bit, reflect on your kids' time in school, and start discussing where to go from here. Depending on age and ability level, appropriately involve them in processing and talking about their school experience. Get good intel.

- **Refuel.** It is essential for us parents to deschool ourselves before making big homeschool plans and curriculum purchases. It's putting on your oxygen mask first before helping others find theirs. We gain clarity, regain our own sense of purpose, and pave the way for a truly transformative educational experience for our children. It can be a challenge, but the reward is *so* worth the work!

Absorb a buffet of ideas and opinions to see which ones are the most appetizing to you. Start by reading books from powerful voices that sing your same song. I have a free download of some of my personal favorite reads that were game-changers for me. That's on my website christy-faith.com if you'd like to have a good list to start with. (And, psst! You're already reading this book. You're well on your way down the deschooling road!)

- **Dream.** Close your eyes and imagine the ideal educational journey for your child. An environment that aligns with your values and celebrates your child's unique strengths and interests. Curriculum that sparks their curiosity, nurtures their love for learning, and empowers them to think critically and creatively. Flexible and personalized that allows for exploration and growth. Write this stuff down because you can make it a reality.

- **Question.** Examine and question some of the core beliefs stamped in our minds from the traditional school system. If you've spent any amount of time in or around the traditional school system, you are likely affected by its influence, much like I was. Key is how you plan to assess your child's progress. I asked this question in an earlier chapter, but it's worth revisiting: if your child works harder than you've ever seen them work before on a subject, it can mean the world to them if you praise their effort.

- **Bond.** Spending intentional time every day with your child is essential for deschooling. This is a precious opportunity to reconnect as a family and relate with your kids at a deeper level. Deschooling goes beyond academics; it's about forging a deep, profound connection with your child, establishing trust, and nurturing their innate love for learning and well-being. In essence, deschooling is a holistic journey that encompasses not only your child's education, but also your own personal and relational growth.

- **Assess.** Take a high-level overview of your child's current educational experience. Record any concerns you may have regarding their academics, social health, or overall fulfillment within the system. Consider your child's academic growth, social interactions, extracurricular activities, and overall happiness with their school experience. Note areas where you feel confident and successful, as well as where you do not. If currently homeschooling, reflect on your homeschooling journey and honestly evaluate where you stand.

- **Be Unschooly.** Deschooling is not passively escaping or just checking out, but a period of relaxed learning, interest-led learning, and even unschooling, depending on what your family needs, or is of value. Reclaiming your child's education is about reclaiming their love for learning. What will that take for your family?

As stated earlier, I generally recommend a more gentle approach covering the 3Rs and embracing a more interest-led approach with other subjects, but you don't have to do that. How you deschool, and what you do during this time is your decision.

Check out fun, interesting places in your area. Historical buildings, museums, landmarks, art galleries, business

In essence, deschooling is a holistic journey that encompasses not only your child's education, but also your own personal and relational growth.

incubators, manufacturing facilities, fashion stores, the list goes on and on! Bury your noses in some great books. Play games as a family. Read aloud. Watch documentaries. Go to concerts, sporting events, and charity events. Take kids to the library and let them read what they want as long as they want. It's time to turn learning into play again! Take a close look at how your child answers the 20 questions in the next section. Their answers are clues for creating an amazing season of memories.

20 Questions to Kickstart Your Deschooling Adventure (for Newbies and Homeschool Veterans Alike)

Many parents have told me, "'Christy, I'm not sure where to begin!" The following 20 questions are for you and your child to explore during the deschooling phase. These questions apply whether you're just starting out with homeschooling or have been homeschooling for a while and simply want to up-level your homeschooling game. After each question, I've included a note on the valuable insights you can gain from your child's response. For a free worksheet version for your kids to complete, without the parent note, and with designated space for their answers, please visit christy-faith.com. Here are the questions:

1. What's your favorite thing we do as a family? (Discovering activities that promote family bonding and joy,

which can be incorporated into the homeschooling experience.)

2. What's one adventure you wish we could do together? (Identifying shared interests and potential learning opportunities that align with the child's preferences.)

3. If a blind person wanted to know what you're like, how would you want someone to describe you *without* saying anything about how you look? (Encouraging the child to reflect on their non-physical attributes, fostering self-awareness and self-esteem.)

4. If you could describe in one word how you feel about school up till now, what would that word be? (Providing a succinct expression of the child's emotional connection to their previous school experience, which can inform a more tailored homeschooling approach.)

5. If you could use only one word to describe what you want school to feel like a year from now, what would that one word be? (Setting a vision and emotional tone for the desired homeschooling environment.)

6. Is there anything you really want to learn more about that we can learn together? (Uncovering specific interests and preferences for collaborative learning experiences between parent and child.)

7. Would you rather read a book, listen to a book, or watch a play or presenter share about that book? (Identifying preferred learning modalities and providing insight into how to engage your child effectively.)

8. What's your least favorite part about school? What's your favorite part about school? (Understanding

aspects of the school environment that were challenging or enjoyable, which can guide you in tailoring the
homeschooling approach.)

9. Would you rather use a whiteboard, a science lab, or
a paintbrush? (Exploring preferred learning tools and
environments, aiding in the creation of a conducive
learning space.)

10. If you had a magic wand, what's the most challenging part about school that you would make the easiest? (Highlighting areas of struggle for the child, which
can guide you in providing additional support or
resources.)

11. If you could go back in time for a day, what part of
history would you want to explore and why? (Revealing historical interests and curiosities that can be integrated into the homeschooling curriculum.)

12. Who is your favorite author or what is your favorite
story? (Identifying literary preferences, which can
inform the selection of reading materials.)

13. What did you like about your favorite teacher or what
do you like about my teaching? (Understanding the
qualities and teaching style that resonate with the
child, providing insights for your role as an educator.)

14. What did you dislike about your least favorite teacher
or what do you wish was different about my teaching?
(Identifying aspects of teaching style or behavior that
the child finds challenging or ineffective, allowing you
to adapt your approach.)

15. When have you felt the most misunderstood? (Encouraging open communication about feelings and experiences, fostering trust and empathy between you and your child.)

16. Describe a time at school or at our homeschool when you felt the most frustrated. (Exploring moments of frustration, offering the parent insight into potential challenges that may need special attention.)

17. Would you rather make new things or fix broken things to be new again? (Discovering creative and problem-solving tendencies, informing hands-on learning activities.)

18. Who inspires you the most and why? (Identifying role models and sources of inspiration, which can be integrated into the child's educational journey.)

19. What type of animal is like your personality? (Drawing parallels between personality traits and animal characteristics, providing a creative and insightful perspective on self-awareness.)

20. If you could develop any skill or hobby, what would it be and why? (Exploring aspirations for personal growth and development, guiding the parent in facilitating opportunities for skill-building and exploration.)

Remember This

- Deschooling helps to de-imprint us from the school system, and to build the clarity, confidence, and courage to thrive in homeschooling.

- Deschooling also helps to minimize the normal, temporary "storming" stage that can be frustrating and discouraging as your "team" forms.

- For a free worksheet version of "20 Questions to Kickstart Your Deschooling Adventure" for your kids to fill out, please visit christy-faith.com.

CHAPTER ELEVEN

You Are Enough

"Armed with love, common sense, and a nearby woodshed, colonial mothers often achieved more than our modern-day elementary schools with their federally-funded programs and education specialists."
—Robert A. Peterson, Headmaster, The Pilgrim Academy[1]

"Christy, what if I . . ."

She paused. I could see the wheels turning, the rest of the sentence stuck in her mind like a forbidden curse. I waited. You could tell she wasn't asking about curriculum, homeschooling style, or what forms to file with her state. No, what came next was the unspoken insecurity stealing the confidence of so many amazing parents.

"What if I'm not . . . enough for my daughter?"

Wide eyes. A brave confession. Brimming with tears. Holding strong, ready to break any second now. The rest of our group sat in silence. Then, a nod. Another head nodding. More parents showing solidarity. The chat starting to fill up with "Girl, I *feel* the same way!" and "You're so brave to ask that. I've been wondering that about myself for years."

233

That's what we want to know, right? That we're enough. That we *do* have what it takes to make this whole parenting thing work. Even thinking about homeschooling may seem like choosing the extra-tough difficulty level on an already challenging journey.

I think it's human to wonder if we're up to the challenge. Not in a *Little Engine That Could* sort of optimism, but in a sleep-snatching, anxiety-shoveling, put-on-a-brave-face type of optimism. Because the stakes are high. It's our kids' future we're talking about here! It's their job prospects, career paths, and likeability with other kids in the neighborhood, on their sports teams, or at the next set of tryouts. It's *all* on the line . . .

And that's where the pressure can be so immense that one bad day can be enough to want to quit, throw on *Legally Blonde,* and work your way through a Häagen-Dazs coffee ice cream bucket. (Hypothetically speaking, for someone who's definitely not me . . .)

Here's the quiet beauty of being a homeschooling parent: You don't have to have it all figured out for the next 12+ years of your child's life. You're not a school district planning for the next decade or two. You have much more flexibility. Just like when you begin parenting, you work through all the stages of babyhood and childhood as they come. Same with homeschooling. Your kids can know you are all on the journey together! You simply need to focus on figuring out today with an eye toward the next year or so.

What's behind the "enoughness" question? First, it's a question of capacity. Do you have the bandwidth to give your child a great education at home?

Discovering groundbreaking resources for your child's education is an exciting journey. In fact, you'll come across curricula that provide detailed scripts designed for teachers in traditional school settings, specifically tailored to your child's level. Rest assured, there are numerous experts who specialize in various subjects, and you can place your trust in their expertise to guide your child's learning experience. With such a wealth of amazing

Envision yourself not as the homeschool teacher, but as the general contractor. Your role is to hire, organize, and orchestrate the team of educators.

resources and knowledgeable individuals available, you can confidently navigate the path of homeschooling with a sense of assurance and support.

Instead of seeing yourself as the teacher in your child's homeschool world, envision yourself as a general contractor. Your role is to hire and organize. A general contractor, orchestrating a team of specialists to construct the foundation of your child's education. As the general contractor you don't have to be *the* expert in every subject. You have the freedom to hire specialists who excel in specific areas and ensure that the overall outcome meets your expectations. And hey, when you find joy and fulfillment in getting your hands dirty and taking on some of the work yourself, that's fantastic too! It's all about finding the right balance and creating an educational environment that best suits your child's needs.

The first part of the "enoughness" question is about capacity, but the second part is about capability. Are you capable of giving your child a great education?

Yes, you are more than enough for what your child needs. It's the celebration that I see so many homeschooling parents share with me every single day:

> "Thanks to homeschooling, my child had the freedom to fully explore their passion for music, allowing them to excel and achieve great success in their musical pursuits."

> "My mom, without a college degree, homeschooled me, and I became a successful entrepreneur, earning multiple six figures running my own business."

> "With the freedom to customize their education, my children developed strong leadership skills and have excelled in their academics, and are college-bound."

> "Homeschooling empowered my family to focus on character development, and now my kids are compassionate, well-rounded individuals who actively make a difference in their communities."

> "Thanks to my homeschooling experience, I made the deliberate choice to prioritize my family by staying at home and homeschool my own children."

> "I barely graduated high school, and yet, all four of my kids graduated high school and were accepted into their dream schools."

These are not exceptions to the norm—I see these types of success stories from parents on this homeschooling adventure from every different walk of life.

Parents who are just like you once wondered, "Am I going to be enough for my child? Am I going to mess this up?"

Parenting is about relationships. No one knows your child like you do. No one knows the best way they learn, what triggers them, what they love doing the most, their personality, and all of the unique quirks and intricacies of your child as you do. Read the following questions slowly.

- Who is the best person to impart your family values to your child? You are.

- Who can provide the safest possible environment to protect against bullying? You can.

- Who can better instill your faith tradition or belief system to your child? You can.

- Who has the commitment to teach subjects and skills not taught in schools? You do.

- Who can foster a deeper, more meaningful connection with your child throughout their school day? You can.

- Who can tailor instruction to fit your child's exact learning style? You can.

- Who is the best at letting your child work at their own learning pace? You are.

- Who has the freedom to choose the exact method by which your child is educated? You do.

- Who can encourage a lifelong love of learning and foster their creativity? You can.

- Who can custom-build their schedule so they're free to pursue a serious sport, skill, or talent? You can.

- Who has the patience, deep understanding of the precise factors and influences, and knows exactly how to best accommodate your child's special needs? You do.

- Who is the most interested in your child avoiding a seven-hour school day and homework because you value precious time? You are!

- Who has a vested interest in creating a unique lifestyle like road-schooling, vacation, or homesteading that will create core memories for the rest of your child's life? You do!

- Who is capable of offering an alternative education style, like Charlotte Mason, classical education, or others in an interest-led way for your child? You are.

- Who can help find healthier friends for your child and you to enjoy? You can.

- Who is the best at preserving your child's innocence and helping them avoid early exposure to mature topics? You are.

- Who can provide physically, mentally, and emotionally safe environments to protect against bullying, school shootings, peer-oriented addictive behavior, and negative mental health challenges? You can.

Why do I give you this list of questions? Because I want this to be what you run back to on those ice cream bucket–digging, mascara-running, yes-Mommy's-sorry-for-yelling days when you wonder if you have what it takes.

Re-read this chapter on the hard and ugly days. Take a photo and save it as your phone's background or tape it to your bathroom mirror. Let this be the small flame that you cup your hands around when the storms of life and second-guessing yourself threaten to snuff out your confidence.

There is no one in the world more capable than you of giving your child everything you want for their education. No one. Don't let anyone tell you otherwise.

There's a good chance you're reading this chapter again, and you're wondering, "Christy, I need *something* to keep going on." Here's the simple truth that I want to whisper to your heart right now . . .

What you truly want for your child is a gift only you can provide.

There is no better place to be educated than in a loving home with a motivated parent.

As you embark on your homeschooling journey, let the title of this book, *Homeschool Rising*, resonate deeply within you. Embrace the fact that you are part of a rising movement, driven by parents who are determined to provide their children with an education that goes beyond textbooks and test scores.

With every lesson, milestone, and breakthrough, remember you are not alone. Homeschooling is a powerful choice, and it is in the hands of parents like you that the true potential of education is realized. Embrace this incredible journey, knowing you are shaping the minds, hearts, and futures of your children in a way that no other setting can replicate.

Homeschool rising indeed, and it is your love, dedication, and unwavering belief that fuel its ascent.

Remember This

- Education is about igniting a flame; and as the most important person in your child's life, a parent, is the best one to ignite it.

- You are your child's strongest advocate; don't relinquish this responsibility, think someone else can do it better, or let anyone take it from you.

- For tools to unlock a new level of homeschool confidence and a hub to "find your people" visit Christy-Faith.com.

About the Author

Christy-Faith is an education expert with over 20 years of professional experience in K–college academics and administration. She has trained teachers, mentored parents, and instructed and guided a wide variety of students, including those who are gifted, individuals with wide ranges of challenges/diagnoses, differently wired learners, and those who are twice exceptional (2E).

She now applies her deep experience in education to advocate for homeschooling and help and encourage countless homeschool parents—both new and veteran—to take the leap, remain steadfast, and revitalize their purpose.

After beginning her education career in the classroom and as a private tutor, she and her husband established a private learning center. Becoming known for highly individualized instruction and impressive academic outcomes, their center grew into one of the most successful private learning centers in the country.

When her own children approached school age, she had an awakening to the value of homeschooling that profoundly transformed her perspective on educating children. She and her husband sold their learning center and turned to applying their knowledge and expertise in education to mentor and support parents along their homeschooling journey.

When she's not encouraging parents on social media, Christy advises them within her flourishing Thrive Homeschool Community, her podcast The Christy-Faith Show, and writing. All while imperfectly educating her four "endlessly entertaining" children alongside her husband, Scott, in Colorado.

Notes

Chapter 1: The Most Dangerous Question: What Makes for a Great Education?

1. Gray, P. (2013*). Free to Learn: Why Unleashing the Instinct to Play Will Make Our Children Happier, More Self-Reliant, and Better Students for Life*. Basic Books, p. 80.

2. Pope, Denise Clark. (2003). *Doing School: How We Are Creating a Generation of Stressed-Out, Materialistic, and Miseducated Students*. Paperback. Yale University Press.

3. Ibid., p. 4.

4. Frederick Douglas quotes. (n.d.). BrainyQuotes. Retrieved September 3, 2023, from https://www.brainyquote.com/quotes/frederick_douglass_201574

5. Yale Center for Emotional Intelligence and the Yale Child Study Center. (2020, April). "High School Students' Feelings: Discoveries from a Large National Survey and an Experience Sampling Study."

6. Lathrap, M. T. (1895). Judge softly. In Poems (pp. 9–10). Jackson, MI: Mary T. Lathrap. Retrieved November 12, 2023, from https://www.aaanativearts.com/walk-mile-in-his-moccasins

7. Brown, Brené. (2019). *Braving the Wilderness: The Quest for True Belonging and the Courage to Stand Alone*. Random House, p. 63.

8. Gallup. (2022, September 1). "Americans' Satisfaction with K–12 Education on Low Side." Retrieved September 3, 2023, from https://news.gallup.com/poll/399731/americans-satisfaction-education-low-side.aspx

Chapter 2: The Homeschool Revolution: Why Parents Are Pulling Out Their Kids in Droves

1. https://www.thoughtco.com/mark-twain-education-2832664

2. https://www.solutionsbysss.com/blog/are-private-schools-ahead-of-public-schools/

3. Ibid.

4. https://www.nheri.org/how-many-homeschool-students-are-there-in-the-united-states-during-the-2021-2022-school-year/

5. https://nces.ed.gov/nhes/data/2019/pfi/cbook_pfi_pu.pdf

6. U.S. Census Bureau. https://www.census.gov/library/stories/2021/03/homeschooling-on-the-rise-during-covid-19-pandemic.html

7. Ibid.

8. https://www.theatlantic.com/education/archive/2016/03/homeschooling-without-god/475953/

9. https://nces.ed.gov/programs/coe/indicator/tgk/homeschooled-children

10. https://www.census.gov/library/stories/2021/03/homeschooling-on-the-rise-during-covid-19-pandemic.html

11. https://dcas.dmdc.osd.mil/dcas/app/summaryData/deaths/byYearManner

12. Irwin, V., Wang, K., Cui, J., and Thompson, A. (2022). "Report on Indicators of School Crime and Safety: 2021 (NCES 2022-092/NCJ 304625)." National Center for Education Statistics, U.S. Department of Education, and Bureau of Justice Statistics, Office of Justice Programs, U.S. Department of Justice. Washington, DC. Retrieved 8/30/2023 from https://nces.ed.gov/pubsearch/pubsinfo.asp?pubid=2022092. https://nces.ed.gov/pubs2022/2022092.pdf

13. https://time.com/5550803/depression-suicide-rates-youth/

14. https://news.stanford.edu/2014/03/10/too-much-homework-031014/

15. Cooper, H., Robinson, J. C., and Patall, E. A. (2006). "Does Homework Improve Academic Achievement? A Synthesis of Research, 1987–2003." *Review of Educational Research, 76*(1), 1–62. And Maltese, A. V., Tai, R. H., and Fan, X. (2012). "When Is Homework Worth the Time? Evaluating the Association between Homework and Achievement in High School Science and Math." *The High School Journal, 96*(1), 52–72.

16. https://www.nationaljewish.org/about/news/press-releases/2016/homeschool-sleep

17. https://www.ncbi.nlm.nih.gov/pmc/articles/PMC7177233/

18. https://nces.ed.gov/programs/coe/indicator/tgk/homeschooled-children?tid=300#:~:text=More%20than%20two%2Dthirds%20of,on%20family%20life%20together%20

19. U.S. CDC. https://www.prb.org/resources/suicide-replaces-homicide-as-second-leading-cause-of-death-among-u-s-teenagers/. Also, I recommend reading through Hansen and Lang's 2011 published article "Back to School Blues: Seasonality of Youth Suicide and the Academic Calendar" in the *Economics of Education Review, 30*, 850–851 for even more evidence. It can be found at https://www.sciencedirect.com/science/article/abs/pii/S0272775711000677

20. https://www.psychologytoday.com/us/blog/freedom-learn/ 201805/children-s-teens-suicides-related-the- school-calendar

21. https://www.psychologytoday.com/us/blog/freedom-learn/ 201805/children-s-teens-suicides-related-the-school-calendar

22. https://www.cdc.gov/healthyyouth/data/yrbs/pdf/YRBS_Data-Summary-Trends_Report2023_508.pdf

23. https://www.hhs.gov/about/news/2022/03/14/new-hhs-study-jama-pediatrics-shows-significant-increases- children-diagnosed-mental-health-conditions-2016-2020.html

24. https://www.breitbart.com/education/2021/11/22/harvard-study-homeschoolers-generally-become-well-adjusted-responsible-young-adults/

25. https://www.nheri.org/home-school-researcher-socialization-of-home-schooled-children-a-self-concept-study/

26. Drenovsky, C. K., &and Cohen, I. (2012). "The Impact of Home-schooling on the Adjustment of College Students." *International Social Science Review*, *87*(1/2), 19–34. https://www.semanticscholar .org/paper/The-Impact-of-Homeschooling-on-the-Adjustment-of -Drenovsky-Cohen/f2fcc3633216acbcde738f756800e6a587965653

27. Payne, K. J., and Ross, L. M. (2009). *Simplicity parenting: Using the extraordinary power of less to raise calmer, happier, and more secure kids.* New York, Ballantine Books., p. 8.

28. Ibid., p. 9.

29. Ibid., p. 12.

30. U.S. Dept. of Education. (2015). https://www.publicschoolreview .com/blog/why-82-of-public-schools-are-failing

31. Ibid.

32. http://www.statisticbrain.com/number-of-american-adults-who-cant-read/

33. https://www.nationsreportcard.gov/mathematics/supportive_files/2022_rm_press_release.docx

34. Ibid.

35. https://www.nheri.org/home-school-researcher-home-school-graduates-and-their-mothers-talk-about-literacy-instruction/

36. https://www.nheri.org/research-facts-on-homeschooling/

37. https://files.eric.ed.gov/fulltext/ED556234.pdf

38. https://files.eric.ed.gov/fulltext/ED556234.pdf

39. http://icher.org/blog/?p=844

40. https://files.eric.ed.gov/fulltext/ED556234.pdf

41. https://www.nheri.org/home-educated-doing-well-at-college-research-by-michael-cogan/

42. The *whole language approach* is a philosophy of teaching reading that focuses on making students use context cues to guess the meaning of words. It has since been discredited, having no scientific support for its effectiveness. More effective phonics-based methods emphasize instruction for decoding and spelling. For a more detailed explanation, visit https://en.wikipedia.org/wiki/Whole_language#cite_note-18

43. https://news.gallup.com/poll/510401/education-satisfaction-ties-record-low.aspx

44. https://www.breitbart.com/education/2021/11/22/harvard-study-homeschoolers-generally-become-well-adjusted-responsible-young-adults/

45. https://news.yale.edu/2020/01/30/national-survey-students-feelings-about-high-school-are-mostly- negative#:~:text=and%20%E2%80%9Cbored.%E2%80%9D-,In%20a%20nationwide%20survey%20of%2021%2C678%20U.S.%20high%20school%20students,related%20to%20school%20were%20negative.

46. *Intrinsic motivation* is being motivated from within, by the sense of satisfaction and/or joy obtained in performing a task.

47. Ray, B. D. (2004). "Homeschooling Grows Up." *Peabody Journal of Education*, 79(1), 11–22. doi: 10.1207/s15327930pje7901_03

48. https://www.psychologytoday.com/us/blog/freedom-learn/ 201805/children-s-teens-suicides-related-the-school-calendar

Chapter 3: In Plain Sight: The Juicy History and Enduring Legacy of Public Schooling

1. https://illinoisfamily.org/education/the-greatest-threat-to-our-children/

2. Race Forward (n.d.). "Classical Education in America. Historical Timeline of Public Education in the US." Retrieved September 2, 2023, from https://www.raceforward.org/reports/education/historical-timeline-public-education-us

3. Chen, G. (2023, August 24). "A Relevant History of Public Education in the United States." Retrieved September 22, 2023, from https://www.publicschoolreview.com/blog/a-relevant-history-of-public-education-in-the-united-states

4. Teich, M., and Porter, R. (1996). *The Industrial Revolution in National Context; Europe and the USA.* Cambridge University Press, p. 45. https://www.cambridge.org/us/universitypress/subjects/history/european-history-after-1450/industrial-revolution-national-context-europe-and-usa?format=PB&isbn=9780521409407

5. https://usa.usembassy.de/etexts/democrac/16.htm

6. Carl, J. (2009). "Industrialization and Public Education: Social Cohesion and Social Stratification." In Cowen, R., Kazamias, A.M. (eds.), *International Handbook of Comparative Education. Springer International Handbooks of Education*, vol. 22. Springer, Dordrecht. https://doi.org/10.1007/978-1-4020-6403-6_32

7. https://link.springer.com/chapter/10.1007/978-1-4020-6403-6_32#citeas

8. K12 Academics. (n.d.). "Origin of Prussian Education System." Retrieved September 2, 2023, from https://www.k12academics .com/Education Worldwide/Education in Germany/History/Prussian Education System/origin

9. Addresses to the German Nation. (1807), Second Address: "The General Nature of the New Education" (1922). Chicago and London, The Open Court Publishing Company, p. 20. https://archive.org/ details/addressestothege00fichuoft/page/20/mode/2up

10. SciHi. (2019, June 22). "Wilhelm von Humboldt and the Reform of Prussia's Education System." SciHi Blog. Retrieved September 3, 2023, from http://scihi.org/wilhelm-von-humboldt/

11. Karseth, B., Solbrekke, T.D. (2016). "Curriculum Trends in European Higher Education: The Pursuit of the Humboldtian University Ideas." In Slaughter, S., Taylor, B. (eds.), *Higher Education, Stratification, and Workforce Development. Higher Education Dynamics*, vol 45. Springer, Cham. https://doi.org/10.1007/978-3-319-21512.-9_11

12. If you'd like to read further on the Prussian education system, check out James van Horn Melton's work *Absolutism and the Eighteenth-Century Origins of Compulsory Schooling in Prussia and Austria* (2003).

13. Colonial Williamsburg. (n.d.). "Every Man Able to Read: Literacy in Early America." CW Journal. https://research.colonialwilliamsburg .org/Foundation/journal/Winter11/literacy.cfm

14. Personal Account of Horace Mann's Visit to the Schools of Prussia. (2017, January 1). Docshare.Tips. https://docshare.tips/personal-account-of-horace-manns-visit-to-the-schools-of-prussia_5882c113b6 d87fb4298b4674.html

15. Ibid.

16. https://www.mackinac.org/2035

17. https://www.azquotes.com/author/3918-John_Dewey

18. https://tfpstudentaction.org/blog/a-brief-history-of-progressive-education

19. https://tfpstudentaction.org/blog/a-brief-history-of-progressive-education

20. Levin, M. (2021, July 13). *American Marxism*. Threshold Editions.

21. Newman, A. (2021, March 13). "How John Dewey Used Public 'Education' to Subvert Liberty." Retrieved September 8, 2023, from https://illinoisfamily.org/education/how-john-dewey-used-public-education-to-subvert-liberty/

22. Blumenfeld, S. (n.d.). "John Dewey's Plan to Dumb-Down America." Alpha-Phonics. https://alpha-phonics.weebly.com/uploads/2/4/6/5/24650255/181591329-john-dewey-s-plan-to-dumb-down-america-the- primary-education-fetich-forum-1898.pdf, (page 3)

23. Ibid., p. 1.

24. Ibid., p. 12.

25. Gates, F. T. (n.d.). "The Country School of Tomorrow." Internet Archive, p. 6. Retrieved September 3, 2023, from https://archive.org/details/countryschooloft00gates. Gates was the Chairman of J.D. Rockefeller's General Education Board, which heavily supported and funded Dewey's work.

26. Orton, S. T. (1929). "The 'Sight Reading' Method of Teaching Reading, as a Source of Reading Disability." *Journal of Educational Psychology*, *20*(2), 135–143. https://doi.org/10.1037/h0072112

27. Also at http://www.donpotter.net/pdf/orton-sight-reading-method.pdf (pp. 111–112).

28. Blumenfeld, p. 1.

29. Justia (n.d.). *Wisconsin v. Yoder*, 406 U.S. 205 (1972). Justia U.S. Supreme Court. Retrieved September 4, 2023, from https://supreme.justia.com/cases/federal/us/406/205/.

30. NCES. (2015, November 1). "Teacher Turnover: Stayers, Movers, and Leavers." National Center for Educational Statistics. Retrieved September 3, 2023, from https://nces.ed.gov/programs/coe/indicator/slc

31. Alliance for the Separation of School and State. (n.d.). Politics and Education Don't Mix! Retrieved September 3, 2023, from https://www.sepschool.org/

32. Park, Y. (2015). *In Order to Live: A North Korean Girl's Journey to Freedom* (1st ed.). Penguin Press.

Chapter 4: From Helpful to Harmful: What Changed in Education and Why It Matters

1   Kohn, A. (1993). *Punished by Rewards: The Trouble with Gold Stars, Incentive Plans, A's, Praise, and Other.* Houghton Mifflin Harcourt, p. 3.

2. John Taylor Gatto (1992). *Dumbing Us Down: The Hidden Curriculum of Compulsory Schooling.* New Society Publishers.

3. American Psychological Association. (2021). "Education and Lifelong Learning." In *APA Dictionary of Psychology* (2nd ed.). Washington, DC: American Psychological Association.

4. Brainy Quotes (n.d.). Albert Einstein Quotes. Retrieved September 6, 2023, from https://www.brainyquote.com/quotes/albert_einstein_110208

5. Gatto, *Dumbing Us Down.* Seriously, do yourself a favor and get a copy of his book.

6. Wikiquote (2023, August 6). H.G. Wells, from *The Sleeper Wakes.* Retrieved September 6, 2023, from https://en.wikiquote.org/wiki/H._G._Wells

7. Paraphrased from Walt Whitman's *Leaves of Grass: Academy of American Poets (n.d.). O Me! O Life! Poets.org. Retrieved September 6, 2023, from* https://poets.org/poem/o-me-o-life

8. With due credit to Apple co-founder Steve Wozniak for the concept and design of the first PC electronics.

9. Higgins, B. (2011, October 11). "How Barefoot Teen Steve Jobs Helped Cure 3 Million Blind People." Retrieved September 7, 2023, from https://www.hollywoodreporter.com/business/digital/steve-jobs-cure-blind-246760/

10. Lydgate, C. (2011, December 1). "Obituaries: Visionary Technologist, Prodigal Son." *Reed Magazine*. https://www.reed.edu/reed-magazine/in-memoriam/obituaries/december2011/steve-jobs-1976.html

11. Gray, P. (2009, September 9). "Seven Sins of Our System of Forced Education: Forced Education Interferes with Children's Abilities to Educate Themselves." https://www.psychologytoday.com/us/blog/freedom-learn/200909/seven-sins-our-system-forced-education

12. Quotefancy. (n.d.). Gilbert K. Chesterton. https://quotefancy.com/quote/818325/Gilbert-K-Chesterton-The-only-people-who-seem-to-have-nothing-to-do-with-the-education-of

13. Murphy, R. P. (1998, July 1). The Origins of the Public School. FEE .org. https://fee.org/articles/the-origins-of-the-public- school/#13

14. *Fields v. Palmdale School District PSD* (2005). U.S. Court of Appeals, Ninth Circuit - https://caselaw.findlaw.com/us-9th-circuit/1051665.html

15. Toynbee, A. J. (1947). *A Study of History* (1st American ed.). Oxford University Press.

16. Bartholet, E. (n.d.). "Homeschooling: Parent Rights Absolutism vs. Child Rights to Education & Protection." Retrieved September 6, 2023, from https://arizonalawreview.org/homeschooling-parent-rights-absolutism-vs-child-rights-to-education-protection/

17. Smith, J. M. (n.d.). "HSLDA to Harvard Prof: Homeschooling is a Fundamental Right. HSLDA Responds." https://hslda.org/post/hslda-to-harvard-prof-homeschooling-is-a-fundamental-right#:~:text=Summary,for%2C and educate their children

18. Gatto.

19. Watters, A. (2015, April 25). "The Invented History of 'The Factory Model of Education." Retrieved July 6, 2023, from https://hackeducation.com/2015/04/25/factory-model

20. *Merriam-Webster Dictionary*. (n.d.). Pedagogy. Merriam-Webster Dictionary. Retrieved September 6, 2023, from https://www.merriam-webster.com/dictionary/pedagogy

Chapter 5: The Homeschooling Edge: Where Possibilities Flourish

1. Yeats's defenders would likely claim this thought originated with his writing, but history is nothing if not an echo of ideas curated to imitate originality.

2. Charlotte Mason. *The Original Home Schooling Series.* https://www.amazon.com/Original-Home-Schooling-Charlotte-Mason/dp/160459439X

3. https://en.wikipedia.org/wiki/Maslow'shierarchyofneeds

4. https://en.wikipedia.org/wiki/Abraham_Maslow

5. https://montessori150.org/maria-montessori/montessori-quotes/educate-human-potential-26

6. John Taylor Gatto. (1992). *Dumbing Us Down: The Hidden Curriculum of Compulsory Schooling.* New Society Publishers.

7. Charlotte Mason, *Parents and Children: Charlotte Mason's Original Home Schooling Series,* vol. 2, p. 247. Ambleside Online.

Chapter 6: Understanding Homeschooling: What It Is and Why People Do It

1. Holt, J., and Farenga, P. (2003). *Teach Your Own: The John Holt Book of Homeschooling.* Da Capo Lifelong Books.

2. https://americanaddictioncenters.org/trauma-stressor-related-disorders/effects-being-bullied-harassed

3. https://literacyinc.com/about-us/#:~:text=56%25%20of%20young%20people%20claim,a%20book%20after%20high%20school

Chapter 7: Flipping the Script on Socialization: The Most Common Objection Is Our Greatest Strength

1. Brown, B. (2017). *Braving the Wilderness: The Quest for True Belonging and the Courage to Stand Alone*. Random House.

2. Neufeld, Gordon, and Gabor Maté, Gabor. (2014) *Hold On to Your Kids*, Ballantine Books, p. 7.

3. Ibid., p. 11.

4. Ibid.

5. Ibid., p. 13.

Chapter 8: Hitting the Books: Educational Myths about Homeschooling

1. https://kinginstitute.stanford.edu/king-papers/documents/purpose-education

2. https://scholar.google.com/scholar?q=National+Household+Education+Surveys+Program+(NHES)+2016+NCES&hl=en&assdt=0&asvis=1&oi=scholart

3. Of course, one can always find outliers who, for various reasons, choose to spend more or less time on their studies.

4. As explained in the chapter on socialization, age-segregated learning dumbs down our children's ability to absorb information.

5. https://www.act.org/content/dam/act/unsecured/documents/Info-Brief-2015-2.pdf

6. https://college.harvard.edu/admissions/application-process/application-requirements

Chapter 9: Moving Beyond the Shadow of Doubt: Common Homeschooling Hang-Ups and Fears

1. https://www.nheri.org/research-facts-on-homeschooling/

2. https://www.apa.org/topics/resilience/building-your-resilience

3. https://www.mayoclinic.org/tests-procedures/resilience-training/in-depth/resilience/art-20046311

4. https://hslda.org/post/will-my-teen-miss-out

5. Hill, N. E., and Tyson, D. F. (2009). "Parental Involvement in Middle School: A Meta-Analytic Assessment of the Strategies That Promote Achievement." *Developmental Psychology*, 45(3), 740–763.

6. https://www.nheri.org/research-facts-on-homeschooling/

Chapter 10: Deschooling: Your Bridge over Anxious Waters

1. https://en.wikipedia.org/wiki/Boilingfrog#Citedreferences

2. https://en.wikipedia.org/wiki/Imprinting(psychology)

3. Ibid.

4. Ibid.

5. https://en.wikipedia.org/wiki/Imprinting(organizationaltheory)

6. https://www.simplypsychology.org/pavlov.html

7. Park, Y. (2015). *In Order to Live: A North Korean Girl's Journey to Freedom* (1st ed.). Penguin Press.

8. https://hr.mit.edu/learning-topics/teams/articles/stages-development

9. http://www.davidtinapple.com/illich/1970deschooling.html

10. Gray, P. (2013). *Free to Learn: Why Unleashing the Instinct to Play Will Make Our Children Happier, More Self-Reliant, and Better Students for Life*. Basic Books.

11. https://www.gao.gov/blog/2018/04/10/disciplining-public-school-students

12. https://www.unesco.org/en/articles/what-you-need-know-about-school-violence-and-bullying

Chapter 11: You Are Enough

1. https://fee.org/articles/education-in-colonial-america/

Let's Connect

Head over to Christy-Faith.com for extensive resources to support you on your homeschool journey, including:

FREE How to Homeschool Guide

FREE 5-Minute Homeschool Style Finder

FREE Curriculum Recommendations

FREE 20 Questions to Quickstart Your Deschooling Adventure

FREE Book *Recommendations for Homeschool Parents*

Thrive Homeschool Community—Find all the tools you need to build an undeniably successful homeschool
And follow me on my socials:

https://www.tiktok.com/@Christy_Faith

https://www.instagram.com/Christy_Faith_Homeschool/

https://www.youtube.com/@Christy-Faith

https://www.facebook.com/ChristyFaithHomeschool/

https://www.pinterest.com/ChristyFaithHomeschooling/

Index